POLITICS
of DEATH

WILLIAM M KIRTLEY

ISBN: 1470045400
ISBN-13: 9781470045401
Library of Congress Control Number: 2012902768
CreateSpace, North Charleston, SC

Table of Contents

Part II - Keeping What You Got: Recurring Maintenance
Chapters 5-7

Preface

The art of living well and the art of dying well are one.

Epicurus[1]

I asked Barbara Coombs Lee, one of the authors of Oregon's Death with Dignity Act, if her work with death and dying ever depressed her. She answered that she found her work exhilarating because she learned so much about life. I understand her comment better now after writing this book. I talked to many wonderful people whose stories enriched my life and helped me understand the difficult end-of-life decisions that come to us all.

I remember sitting at the dinner table with my wife, discussing the Oregon Death with Dignity initiative in 1994. Whatever reservations I entertained at the time, I am convinced that much good has come from this unique law. Those who chose to hasten their deaths are grateful at being able to make this choice. Physicians in Oregon discuss a full range of end-of-life options because they know that patients will ask about Death with Dignity.

Years after that dinner table discussion, I found a suitable framework for analysis in political scientist Barbara Nelson's book, *Making An Issue of Child Abuse*.[2] Part I of my book tells the story of how Oregonians adopted a Death with Dignity law. Individual chapters deal with the 1994 campaign, a controversial decision by the Oregon legislature to resubmit the law to the voters, the 1997 campaign, and court decisions that allowed the law to go into effect. Nelson calls this part of the process *initial maintenance*.

She describes efforts to preserve the adoption of an issue as *recurring maintenance*. Coombs Lee notes, "After you pass a law, then you have to roll up your sleeves and work."[3] Part II of this book deals with challenges to Oregon's law in Congress and the federal court system.

Part III details the struggle over Death with Dignity legislation in other states. Chapter 8 chronicles the defeat of initiatives in Michigan and Maine and bills in the legislatures of California, Hawaii, and Vermont. Chapter 9 analyzes adoption by the voters of Washington and the courts of Montana in 2008. Chapter 10, the last chapter, evaluates scientific studies and the annual report of the Oregon Department of Human Services (DHS).

I documented each chapter extensively, because partisans contest every aspect of the debate. Interviews with key players helped me understand the moral commitment that generates such passion. This fervor moves both sides to control the meaning of words. My use of a particular terminology implies neither dissent nor assent.

Early reviewers of this manuscript encouraged me to appeal to a larger audience. For this reason, I included the stories of those who legally hastened their deaths and used a narrative approach to analyze the conflicts between the antagonists. In the process, I returned to the origins of this work, a dinner table discussion that helped two people make an informed decision on a vital issue.

Cast of Characters

I. Proponents

A. Groups

Friends of Al Sinnard formed the Oregon Right to Die Committee in 1993. This group spearheaded the successful campaign for the Oregon Death with Dignity Act in 1994.

Oregon Death with Dignity: Founded in 1997 to lead the campaign in the second successful election for the Oregon Death with Dignity Act.

Compassion and Dying Federation: Founded in Seattle, Washington (1993) to provide national leadership in improving pain management and end-of-life choices to include aid in dying for terminally ill, mentally competent adults.

The Death with Dignity National Center: Founded in 1994 to advocate for end-of-life choices and replication of the Oregon law, headquarters in Portland, Oregon.

Oregon Compassion in Dying: Organized in 1997 after passage of the Oregon Death with Dignity Act to facilitate implementation of the Act and provide information on end-of-life options.

Compassion & Choices: Formed in 2004 as a result of a merger of the Compassion in Dying Federation and End of Life Choices, formerly the Hemlock Society, headquarters in Denver, Colorado. Those dissatisfied with the merger formed The Final Exit Network.

Oregon Compassion & Choices: Affiliate of Compassion & Choices.

B. Individuals

Barbara Coombs Lee: President, Compassion & Choices, attorney and nurse, member of Sinnard's Group, chief petitioner for the initiative petition, intervenor-appellant in *Lee v. Oregon* (1994).

George Eighmey: Served three terms in Oregon Legislative Assembly, executive director of Oregon Compassion in Dying and its successor, Oregon Compassion & Choices.

Peter Goodwin: Retired professor Department of Family Medicine, Oregon Health Science & University, member of Hemlock Society and Sinnard's group, chief petitioner for the initiative petition, and intervenor-appellant in *Lee v. Oregon* (1994). He died 11 March 2012 using the Death with Dignity law.

Derek Humphry: Writer and founder of the Hemlock Society in 1980, left the society to found the Euthanasia Research and Guidance Organization (ERGO) in 1992.

Elven "Al" Sinnard: Retired businessman, founded group that wrote the Oregon Death with Dignity Act, served as chief petitioner for initiative petition, and intervenor-appellant in *Lee v. Oregon* (1994).

Eli Stutsman: Appeals court attorney, worked on Initiative 119 campaign in Washington in 1991, member of Sinnard's group, legal representative for Oregon Death with Dignity, co-counsel *Lee v. Oregon* (1994), *Oregon v. Ashcroft* (2001), and *Gonzales v. Washington* (2006), board president of Death with Dignity National Center.

Kathryn Tucker: Attorney and Director of legal affairs for Compassion & Choices; worked on Initiative 119 campaign in Washington in 1991; counsel in *Compassion in Dying v. Washington* (1994), *Oregon v. Ashcroft* (2001), and *Washington v. Glucksberg* (1997); argued *Gonzales v. Washington* (2006) before the Supreme Court; litigator on behalf of the patients and physicians.

II. Opponents of the Death with Dignity Act

A. Groups

Physicians for Compassionate Care: Founded after the passage of the Oregon Death with Dignity Act in 1994 to oppose such legislation and promote compassionate care for severely ill patients.

B. Individuals

Charles Bentz: President Physicians for Compassionate Care, Providence Health Care System.
Robert Castagna: Lobbyist for the Oregon Catholic Conference.
N. Greg Hamilton: Practicing psychiatrist, cofounder and senior scholar for Physicians for Compassionate Care.
William Levada: Served as Archbishop of Portland in 1986, appointed Archbishop of San Francisco in 1995, appointed Prefect of the Congregation for the Doctrine of the Faith in Rome, elevated to the cardinalate in 2006.
Kenneth Stevens: Professor Department of Radiation Oncology, Oregon Health & Science University, cofounder, Physicians for Compassionate Care.
Bill Toffler: Professor Department of Family Medicine, Oregon Health Science & University, cofounder and national director, Physicians for Compassionate Care.

Part I - Getting What You Want:

Initial Maintenance

Chapters 1-4

Chapter I

Mavericks and Pioneers: The Election of 1994

Introduction

Sara, Al Sinnard's wife of forty-nine years, suffered unremitting, untreatable pain after undergoing two open-heart surgeries. She told her husband, "I want out."[4] Their minister at the Unitarian Church suggested they contact the Hemlock Society. The day after Sara received information from the Society, she commented, "I can do it. I've got a choice."[5] She put a plastic bag over her head and died of suffocation on October 7, 1989. Al waited outside the room. Legal advice he received made it clear that authorities could charge him with murder if he actively helped his wife die. Tears came to his eyes whenever he remembered her death. "I couldn't be with her when she died, and that's not right."[6]

Sinnard was a man of compassionate heart and a levelheaded businessperson. He applied his considerable organizational skills to spare others the pain and anguish he bore over the death of his wife.[7] He sold his chain of card shops in 1990 so that he could work full-time for a law that allowed people to die peaceably in the company of their loved ones. He organized the group that wrote the Oregon Death with Dignity Act.

Sinnard met with a group of people in the basement of his home, starting in December 1990. Members of the group included the following: Eli Stutsman, an attorney who became the driving force of the group; Peter Goodwin, a physician; Mark Trinchero, an attorney whose brother died of acquired immune deficiency syndrome (AIDS); Cheryl Smith, founder of the Portland Chapter of the Hemlock Society; and Myriam Coppens, a nurse.

Sinnard's band of activists considered lobbying Oregon's Legislative Assembly for right-to-die legislation. However, socially conservative Republicans wielded considerable power in the legislature, and lobbyists from the Roman Catholic Church (hereafter referred to as the Church) enjoyed unprecedented access to legislators. The group decided the best chance for success lay in an initiative petition.

There Ought to Be a Law

Several of the people who met in Sinnard's basement belonged to the Hemlock Society, the group that placed Initiative 119 on the ballot in Washington in 1991. This measure authorized physicians to hasten the death of terminal patients by lethal injection. It enjoyed strong initial support, but opposition from the Church and the medical community doomed it to defeat. The California electorate nearly passed a similar measure in 1992, despite ads that depicted nurses giving lethal injections to comatose patients.

Smith drafted a measure similar to the Washington and California initiatives. She argued that lethal prescriptions excluded those who could not swallow and that lethal injections provided the safest way to hasten death.[8] Stutsman, based on his experience in Washington, proposed an initiative that restricted the role of the physician to writing a prescription.

Goodwin agreed that patients and physicians expressed little interest in lethal injections. He focused on the fact that physicians were illegally prescribing lethal doses of medication. Several studies indicated physicians help patients that ask for aid in dying. Goodwin recounted his shock the first time a patient made such a request. "I felt as if my blood froze."[9] He believed that legalizing lethal prescriptions with safeguards set a standard of care for a practice that occurred across the country.

Sinnard's friends incorporated as the Oregon Right to Die Committee in the spring of 1993. Soon thereafter, Derek Humphry, founder of the Hemlock Society, invited Stutsman to a meeting at the Unitarian Church in Eugene, Oregon. At the meeting, Humphry strongly urged the inclusion of lethal injection in the proposed initiative.[10]

Coombs Lee, a lawyer and a nurse, joined the Committee as a result of an ad Sinnard placed in the Unitarian Church bulletin. Stutsman commented, "If there was any one person I wanted there, it was Barbara."[11] She ensured the language of the initiative petition was compatible with the advance directive law that she crafted as a legislative aide in the Oregon Legislative Assembly. Legislators passed that bill with the understanding that it was the last right-to-die legislation they would consider.

The Committee decided in the fall of 1993 to provide only for legal lethal prescriptions in their proposed initiative. They added safeguards like age and residency requirements. Only physicians who treated terminal illnesses could write lethal prescriptions.[12] They included a prohibition against euthanasia that distanced themselves from Humphry and the Hemlock Society.

Polls showed that the public trusted nurses, physicians, and family members when it came to end-of-life decisions. The Committee chose Coombs Lee, a nurse; Goodwin, a physician; and Sinnard, a bereaved family member, as chief petitioners. They filed the measure on the last day they could submit it, 19 December 1993.[13]

Humphry and Robert Castagna of the Oregon Catholic Conference learned the contents of the initiative on that same day.[14] Humphry, furious that it did not provide for lethal injection, asked for the return of the money he gave the Committee for their first newsletter. Archbishop William Levada of Portland and Bishop Connolly of Baker asked every Catholic in Oregon to contribute $50 to defeat "a euthanasia initiative."[15] "We make this exceptional request because of the seriousness of this proposed initiative."[16]

Phil Keisling (D), Oregon Secretary of State, requested proponents and opponents of the measure for input in writing the official summary of the measure that appears on the ballots and in the Voters' Pamphlet. The two groups disagreed on whether the title should refer to "Physician-Assisted Suicide" or "Death with Dignity." Keisling chose the title "Death with Dignity." Opponents challenged his choice in the Oregon Supreme Court. The Court approved the following title and summary of Measure No. 16 in April 1994.

Table 1.1 Oregon Death with Dignity Act (Measure 16)[17]

Allows terminally ill adults to obtain prescription for lethal drugs.

BALLOT QUESTION: Shall the law allow terminally ill adult Oregon patients the voluntary, informed choice to obtain physician's prescription for drugs to end life?

SUMMARY: Allows terminally ill adult patients the voluntary, informed choice to obtain a physician's prescription to end life. Removes criminal penalties for physician-assisted suicide. Applies when physicians predict patient's death within six months.

Requires: fifteen day waiting period; two oral, one written request; second physician's opinion; counseling if either physician believes patient has mental disorder or impaired judgment from depression. Person has choice whether to notify next of kin. Health care providers are immune from civil or criminal liability for good faith compliance.

Once the Court approved this title and summary, supporters could circulate petitions. Castagna doubted they could collect enough signatures.[18] The Committee hired signature gatherers and easily met the standard 67,000 signatures necessary to qualify for the ballot by 8 July 1994.[19] The Secretary of State certified Measure 16 eight days later.[20]

The Election of 1994

Both sides in the battle over Measure 16 realized the significance of the proposed initiative. Nowhere else in the world was it legal for physicians to help terminally ill patients end their lives. This moral and ethical issue thrust Oregon into the vicissitudes of the cultural wars.

Opponents of Measure 16

Opponents organized two committees, the Coalition for Compassionate Care and Catholics for Compassionate Care, to fight the Oregon Death with Dignity Act. The leadership of both groups and 59.3 percent of the money for the campaign came from the Catholic Church. Seventy dioceses contributed funds. Over 13,000 Oregon Catholics gave $280,000. Two Catholic hospitals in Washington contributed $15,000. Opponents of Measure 16 raised more than $1.5 million, much of it spent on last-minute advertising.[21]

Levada explained to his fellow bishops that the coalition focused its advertising on what polling indicated were the measure's weaknesses: lack of adequate safeguards, potential for abuse, failure to require family notification, and lack of adequate evaluation for depression.[22] An article in the Catholic public affairs magazine *Commonweal* noted that Dr. Jack Kevorkian's first patient, the national headquarters of the Hemlock Society, and Humphry all hailed from Oregon. The author predicted that the issue would remain "divisive in our culture for many years to come."[23]

Proponents of Measure 16

Oregon Death with Dignity, the Oregon Right to Die Committee, and Portland voters raised $546,362.10.[24] A large number of individuals made small contributions. Convinced that Measure 16 was better than the status quo, Humphry changed his mind. He donated $500 and wrote several letters soliciting funds for the campaign.[25] "Why Don't the Busybodies Butt Out and Allow Us to Make Our Own Minds Up," a group sponsored by Oregon businessperson Loren Parks, contributed $150,000. Much of Parks's money went to hard-hitting radio advertising directed against the role of the Catholic Church in the campaign. The National Hemlock Society contributed $175,000.[26]

The Campaign

The contentious election campaign of 1994 was mercifully brief. Oregon Right to Die had only enough funds for a short campaign. They counted on widespread public support and their ability to generate free advertising. One poll found robust majorities for the measure among Democrats and Independents, with Republicans evenly divided. By statute, the state elections Department must mail Voters' Pamphlets twenty days before the election. The Committee concentrated their efforts on this period.

Bishops Levada and Connolly asked the pastors in all the parishes of Oregon to preach against Measure 16. The Church's argument was, "We are not the owners of our lives, but trustees with the duty to preserve and use our lives for the glory of God."[27] Rev. Joseph Jacobberger turned the pulpit of the Cathedral over to a physician. Dr. Thomas Pitre insisted that medical advances meant that no one had to die in pain and there was no need for Measure 16.[28] Castagna castigated the Oregon Medical Association for its neutral stand against the initiative. David Reinhard, a columnist for the *Oregonian*, characterized the measure as "do-it-yourself death" and "euthanasia on the installment plan."[29]

Geoff H. Sugarman, spokesperson for the Oregon Right to Die Committee, charged the Catholic hierarchy of "going against the beliefs of its own members" and spending money on a negative and misleading advertising campaign.[30] Levada accused the Committee of "selling murder in the name of mercy."[31] The Committee hired security guards to protect campaign headquarters after they received more than a dozen threatening calls. A spokesperson for the archdiocese noted that the Church sought only "to promote rational debate and dialogue."[32]

The opponents of Measure 16 circulated a handbill that claimed that the initiative was a euthanasia measure. Stutsman threatened legal action if they didn't pull it. Subsequent advertising took a softer approach.[33] One ad featured a hospice nurse who explained that depression was common in terminally ill patients. She worried that if Measure 16 passed, a patient might hasten his or her death for the wrong reasons.[34]

Oregon Right to Die produced a few powerful paid arguments. They focused on the story of Patti Rosen of Bend, Oregon. She proclaimed, "I am a criminal."[35] Rosen admitted that she gave her daughter, a terminal cancer patient, an illegal lethal dose of drugs. Opponents claimed the argument misrepresented what actually happened. Stutsman replied that, like most ads, "There wasn't time to present the historically correct story."[36]

Polls commissioned by supporters of Measure 16 showed that the Church enjoyed a favorable reputation. They knew that attacks against the Church would provoke a backlash. An ad called "Faces" challenged the Church and emphasized the theme of choice. It depicted the faces of eight females and six males that faded in and out of the picture. The narrator delivered the message that "I don't need government. I don't need any church playing politics with my choices, with my life. I'll decide how and when and in what way I will end my life."[37]

Oregonians rely on the state Voters' Pamphlet to provide them with information on candidates and issues. Supporters of Measure 16 paid $500 apiece for arguments that emphasized the importance of personal choice and repeated the Rosen story. Opponents countered with statements from doctors, hospice nurses, and the emotional story of Connie Harris of Rogue River, Oregon. Harris related her battle with breast cancer and how she enjoyed each day of her life, "days I might never have enjoyed if I had the choice of assisted suicide."[38]

The editors of the statewide newspaper, the *Oregonian*, came out against Measure 16. Proponents of the Oregon Death with Dignity Act paid attention to reporters' questions and fought back with press conferences and press releases. They used touching stories of the dying to lay the groundwork for acceptance of the words they used to frame the issue. As a result, much of the day-to-day reporting on the contest was positive.

An exception to this generally favorable coverage occurred a week before the election. Mark O'Keefe of the *Oregonian* wrote an article that tied Derek Humphry, the "Founding Father" of the assisted-suicide movement, to Measure 16. O'Keefe alluded to Humphry's description of how to kill yourself with a "slug of vodka, a handful of barbiturates and a plastic bag over your head."[39] He repeated allegations that Humphry smothered his first wife, abandoned his second, and divorced his third.[40] A tombstone, sketched at the top of the page, highlighted the story. Coombs Lee lamented that it was too late to counterbalance such powerful images.[41]

This article reinforced the Oregon Right to Die Committee's decision to distance itself from Humphry. Stutsman believed it was the only way supporters convinced the Oregon Medical Association to take a neutral stand on Measure 16.[42] Coombs Lee argued that "Measure 16 was not designed to satisfy the fringe element on either side of the issue, not Derek Humphry and not the archbishop."[43]

The Vote

The election took place on Tuesday, 8 November 1994. Of those that voted, 627,980 (51 percent) favored Measure 16, and 596,018 (49 percent) opposed it. Fifty-seven percent of the registered voters cast their ballots, one-fifth by absentee ballot.[44] This victory came despite its controversial nature. Levada observed, "I'm glad my 89-year-old mother didn't accept my invitation to move to Oregon."[45]

Political analysts gave several reasons for Oregon's approval of the Death with Dignity Act. Levada's fiery rhetoric and visible role made him a target for attacks by the opposition. He precipitated an antireligion backlash in one of the most secular states in the nation. The Catholic Church claims only 10 percent of Oregon's population. Fewer Oregonians identify with any church than in other states. Only about 32.2 percent of Oregon residents attend church regularly, as opposed to 40 or 50 percent in other parts of the nation.[46]

The Portland metropolitan area provided the margin of victory. Voters in rural counties in Eastern and Southern Oregon did not support the measure. Robert Sahr and Susan Banducci, political scientists at Oregon State University, conducted a poll that indicated that 67 percent of the liberals supported the law, as did 57 percent of the moderates, compared to 36 percent of the conservatives.[47] Governor John Kitzhaber (D) approved the concept of the Death with Dignity Act. However, he did not support the measure because he believed there were problems with its implementation and was repulsed by the tactics of both sides in the campaign. He thought the legislature should have corrected what he perceived as defects, before it went to the voters.[48]

Conclusion

The vote was in character for Oregonians, known as mavericks and pioneers. Geoff Sugarman stated: "There is that streak of independence among Oregonians that makes them feel comfortable in passing legislation that has never been done before."[49]

Oregon Right to Die won because they waged a smart, scrappy campaign focused on the issue of choice.[50] The Oregon Death with Dignity Committee framed the issue in words that resonated with Oregonians. They learned from polls and their experience in Washington and California. They knew the opposition and its tactics and stood ready to take advantage of its mistakes. They understood that voters preferred pills to needles. Their decision to distance themselves from Derek Humphry appealed to undecided voters.

Opponents never fathomed why remarks in the Vatican newspaper that described Oregon's law as an "aberrant" and "illegitimate use of the initiative" insulted Oregonians.[51] Levada didn't understand Oregonians or the state's politics. He served in various parishes in the Los Angeles Diocese before becoming Archbishop of Portland in 1986. He based his arguments on information provided by polls rather than offering convincing philosophical or theological arguments as to why the Church believed Measure 16 was wrong.[52]

The neutral stand of the Oregon Medical Association hurt opponents of Death with Dignity. Voters understood that physicians held different opinions on the issue. Dr. William Toffler of Physicians for Compassionate Care admitted that opponents realized too late that Measure 16 was more conservative than previous euthanasia measures and that proponents were extremely well organized. He vowed that his organization would not be caught unaware again.[53]

Dr. Susan Tolle, M.D., of the Center of Ethics in Health Care cited several widely held attitudes that surfaced during the campaign. People believed that medical schools did not adequately train their students in death and dying. Medical professionals did not display sufficient compassion for those near death. The public perceived that many terminal patients suffered needlessly from pain and depression. People maintained that while scientific advances prolonged life, all too often, this meant loss of control for patients.

According to Tolle, passage of Measure 16 served as a "wake-up call" for medical professionals. "It got doctors who hadn't been thinking a lot about the issue paying more attention."[54] The Oregon Health & Science University scheduled additional training in palliative care. The Oregon Medical Association established an end-of-life task force. The legislature passed a bill that gave physicians greater freedom to prescribe large doses of pain medication for the terminally ill.

Opponents brought suit in Eugene Federal District Court. They asked Judge Michael Hogan in *Lee v. Oregon* to issue an injunction preventing the implementation of the Oregon Death with Dignity Act. Hogan agreed with the motion and on 27 December 1994 issued a preliminary injunction that stopped the Act from going into effect.

Proponents deplored the fact that some people would die in pain, while others received illegal assistance from their physicians. They vowed to continue their fight for the right of competent adults to obtain legal lethal prescriptions. Opponents sought help from their allies in the Oregon State Legislative Assembly to overturn or amend the Death with Dignity Act.

Chapter 2

Discordant Discourse:
The Oregon Legislative Assembly

Introduction

Opponents of Death with Dignity understood that, for the most part, Western jurisprudence held that "your life was not yours to dispense with as you pleased."[55] They believed that Judge Hogan's injunction would stand up to review by higher courts. However, they knew that the Supreme Court's impending decision in *Washington v. Glucksberg* could overturn Hogan's decision. For this reason, they attacked the Death with Dignity Act in the 69th Oregon Legislative Assembly.

Hildy Boespflug, a registered nurse from Turner, Oregon, voiced her opposition to the Death with Dignity Act before the Oregon House Judiciary Subcommittee. "My husband is a family practice physician and would not want to become a murderer."[56] She predicted that if the law allowed hastened death for the terminally ill, "divorcees will begin killing themselves over their breakups and teenagers will end their lives for something as simple as a pimple."[57] She suggested a new state motto, "Welcome to Oregon, the suicide state."[58]

Dr. Kenneth Stevens, founder of the newly formed Physicians for Compassionate Care, persuaded the Oregon Medical Association to move from its neutral stance and come out against the Oregon Death with Dignity Act. At that point, Stevens's group, the Oregon Medical Association, Oregon Right to Life, and the Portland Archdiocese "gang tackled" legislators to do something.[59]

The Legislature's Choice: Amend or Repeal

The opposition groups had powerful allies in the legislature. Republicans controlled both houses. Representatives of the socially conservative or moralist wing of the Republican party held positions of leadership and believed it was time to implement their agenda, especially in regard to the Death with Dignity Act.[60] However, their options were limited. Governor Kitzhaber (D) supported the principle of Death with Dignity, although he thought the legislature should amend the Act.[61] He sent the Republican leadership a message that he would veto any attempt to repeal it.[62] As the Republicans lacked the votes to overturn the governor's veto, their only choices were to amend the Act or send it back to the people.

Representative George Eighmey (D-Portland), a right-to-die proponent, also thought that the legislature should correct problems inherent in any new piece of legislation.[63] One of his concerns was the lack of a requirement that a physician attend the death of a patient who ingested a lethal prescription.[64] Judy Uherbelau (D-Ashland) worried about residency requirements. She observed, "We don't want to become a boutique for suicides."[65] Eighmey organized work sessions that included proponents and opponents of the Act. They wrote three bills that included twenty-two amendments to the Act.

House Committee Hearings

The Family Law Committee, a subcommittee of the House Judiciary committee, heard testimony and gathered written comments from 11–13 March 1997. Ron Sunseri (R-Gresham), a religious conservative, chaired the committee. Eighmey served as vice-chair. Members included Charles Starr (R-Hillsboro), Roger Beyer (R-Molalla), Peter Courtney (D-Salem), and Uherbelau. Other legislators attended the hearings and participated although, as unofficial members of the committee, they could not vote.

Penny Schleuter, a Pleasant Hill resident who suffered from ovarian cancer, cautioned the committee to determine who proposed amendments and why. She testified that she believed the Death with Dignity Act needed clarification, but worried that amendments would make it impossible for Oregonians to take advantage of it. She implored committee members to allow the law to go into effect so that people near death could consult with doctors and get help.[66]

Dr. Matt Gruber, a physician from Salem, Oregon, testified that the term "doctor assisted-suicide" did not adequately describe the process outlined under Oregon's Death with Dignity Act. He insisted that amendments would serve as roadblocks to implementation and asked the committee not to consider amendments until after the law went into effect and the Department of Human Services collected data on its use.[67]

N. Greg Hamilton, cofounder of Physicians for Compassionate Care, presented written and oral testimony against Oregon's Death with Dignity Act on 13 March 1997. Representative Jo Ann Bowman (D-Portland) wanted to know why physicians became compassionate and decided to work together to provide alternatives to hastened death only after voters passed the Act.[68] Hamilton replied, "We recognize that not all doctors are compassionate and that is why we need laws."[69]

The committee's discussions centered on amendments that mandated psychological counseling, strengthened residency requirements, required notification of family, provided that a physician must attend the death of a patient, ensured that pharmacists labeled lethal prescriptions as to their purpose, and funded legal lethal prescriptions under the Oregon Health Care Program.

Sunseri reassured his fellow committee members that he sought only to amend the law rather than repeal it or refer it to the voters.[70] Thomas Balmer, the Deputy Attorney General of Oregon, testified that voters would react negatively if they interpreted the attempts of the legislature to amend the Death with Dignity Act as a means of thwarting the results of the election of 1994.[71]

Sunseri told the committee that people asked him about the feasibility of coming to Oregon to find physicians who would write legal lethal prescriptions for them. He asserted that people would die on park benches, at ocean beach waysides, or in hotels.[72] Dr. Philip Levesque, a lobbyist for the American Association of Retired Persons, reassured Sunseri that this would not happen.[73]

At the conclusion of the hearings, Sunseri introduced HB 2954, a bill that referred the Act back to the people as Measure 51. He claimed that the Death with Dignity Act "deals with life and death. If there is ever a law people need to consider with deliberation, this is it."[74] Eighmey admitted his naiveté in thinking that he could work with Sunseri to amend the Act.[75] Several Democrats called Sunseri a liar for saying he wanted to amend the Act, when all along he wanted to sponsor legislation that repealed it.[76]

The editors of the *Oregonian* harbored no illusions about the motives of the social conservatives. "They're not interested in solving these problems. Never were. They're bent on repealing Measure 16."[77] They supported Sunseri's legislation because they believed that the voters did not have all the facts in 1994 and that the ballot, crowded with controversial issues, confused them. These editorial comments presaged the intense debate that followed.

Floor of the House

The debate on the floor of the House commenced with a discussion of the merits of amending or referring the Death with Dignity Act back to the people. Legislators revealed their religious beliefs and told of parents dying in pain for three intense hours. Representative Floyd Prozanski (D-Eugene) spoke of his father, who died of cancer in the summer of 1994. "His death was not with dignity. It was long and drawn-out with suffering and pain."[78] Eighmey suggested that people based end-of-life decisions on moral and religious principles and "that's not what this body is about."[79]

Eighmey introduced a bill amending the Death with Dignity Act to include mandatory counseling, firmer residency safeguards, and a residency requirement. Those advocating repeal of the Act argued that amendments would not fix the Act's flaws. They cited studies from the Netherlands indicating that drugs failed to end patients' lives 25 percent of the time. The House rejected the bill by a 34 to 24 margin.

Representative John Minnis (R-Portland), a police officer in his seventh session in the legislature, conjectured that only lethal injection ensured death without complication and urged an amendment to that effect. He called supporters of hastened death "obnoxious" because they "bristled" at such an amendment.[80] Minnis knew a lethal injection provision would doom the Act at the polls.[81] After three hours of debate, the social conservatives passed Sunseri's bill that asked voters to reconsider the Oregon Death with Dignity Act and sent it to the Senate.

Representative Cynthia Wooten (D-Eugene) asked, "What message are we sending? That the voters don't know what they're doing? That they're stupid?"[82] She predicted the people of Oregon would demonstrate their resentment of the legislature's action by voting overwhelmingly for the Death with Dignity Act. Castagna, of the Oregon Catholic Conference, charged that proponents of the Act finally had to face up to the flaws in their initiative. He warned against appeals to antireligious bigotry and prepared for the upcoming debate in the Senate.[83]

The Oregon Senate

Contentiousness characterized the debate in the Senate. Social conservatives maintained there was no need for the Death with Dignity Act, as modern technology allowed physicians to effectively treat pain. Senator Eileen Qutub (R-Beaverton), a real estate appraiser who received strong support from Oregon Right to Life, held up a large bottle of pills and a plastic bag, claiming that the medication in the bottle would bring about death, but the only sure way to bring about death was to suffocate the patient with the plastic bag.

Marylin Shannon (R-Brooks) insisted that support for such legislation constituted the first step toward euthanasia for the mentally retarded, insane, and elderly, as practiced in Nazi Germany.[84] She argued that pills did not work and that the only way to ensure that patients did not die lingering, painful deaths was to amend the Oregon Death with Dignity Act to provide for lethal injection by a physician.

Supporters of Death with Dignity offered a bill that strengthened residency and counseling requirements. It failed 18 to 12. Senator Kate Brown (D-Portland) emphasized that if the legislature referred the Act to the voters, "The campaign will be about us. It will be about a legislature telling voters they didn't know what they were doing."[85] Shannon disagreed. "It's such a serious vote that I don't think it hurts to send it out to the voters one more time."[86] The bill for referral passed on 9 June 1997 by a 20 to 10 margin.[87] Political analysts found several explanations for the vote.

The vote in the Oregon House of Representatives and Senate followed party lines.

Table 2.1 Party Line Voting on Referral[88]

	House	Senate
Republicans	93% for referral	90% for referral
Democrats	96% against referral	80% against referral

Political analyst Dr. Bill Lunch of Oregon State University argued that once legislators looked at Death with Dignity as a civil rights issue, they took the positions expected of Republicans and Democrats.[89] Uherbelau believed that the blunt talk and moral stance of the conservative wing of the Republican party forced Democrats to close ranks.[90]

Democrats realized that the moralists never seriously considered amending the Death with Dignity Act. They found cohesion in their outrage at Shannon's allusions to Nazi Germany. Representative Bryan Johnston (D-Salem) did not fall neatly into these categories. Johnston, influenced by his Catholic religious roots and a reading of his socially conservative district near Salem, voted with the Republicans to resubmit the Act to the voters.[91]

Senate President Brady Adams (R-Grants Pass) thought that the legislature could discuss issues of death and dying on a mature level, devoid of divisive rhetoric.[92] He was wrong. However, he was correct in his assessment that the only way to maintain party unity was to accede to the demands of the social conservatives.

The legislature authorized a special election for 4 November 1997. Castagna of the Oregon Catholic Conference promised a better funded, more aggressive campaign because of the national public policy potentially at stake.[93] O'Keefe of the *Oregonian* forecast a campaign that would "pit the grassroots networks of Oregon Right to Life against Oregon Right to Die."[94] The election of 1997 was all he predicted—and more.

Conclusion

Opponents of Death with Dignity appealed to social conservatives in the Oregon Legislative Assembly for help. They knew that the moralists stood ready to lead the attack against the Act. The decision of the Ninth Circuit Court of Appeals in *Washington v. Glucksberg* (1997), which established a right to die, lent urgency to this mission. This decision came just three days before the final vote in the Oregon State Senate to refer the Death with Dignity Act back to the people.

The Ninth Circuit Court decision placed the responsibility for deciding the future of Death with Dignity squarely on the shoulders of the legislature. E. J. Dionne, a liberal columnist, observed: "The Court, including its most liberal and its most conservative members, reminded us that we should not use the judiciary to evade democratic debate on difficult questions."[95] The social conservatives knew they had reached a decision point.

Supporters of the Death with Dignity Act were willing to propose amendments to the Act. The social conservatives never seriously entertained the thought of amending the law. Talk of amending it to include lethal injections was a ploy. They believed that any real attempt to amend the Act would make it more viable. Lunch observed, "One of the reasons this came back to the ballot was that the legislative leadership did not like the law. They wanted to just repeal it straight away in the 1997 legislative session rather than fix it."[96]

They thought that their best chance of getting rid of the law was to refer it to the voters, whom they believed would, with more information and time to consider the issue, rescind their previous vote. They failed to take into account the effects of divisive remarks by conservative Republicans. Democrats closed ranks to oppose a second referral of the Death with Dignity Act and predicted grave consequences for the actions of their opponents.

State legislatures are accessible to the people, yet dominated by entrenched lobbyists and immersed in partisan politics. Oregon's legislators represent individual districts, but voters expect them to enact legislation that will benefit all of the state's people. When the members of Oregon's Legislative Assembly thwarted the will of the people, they provoked an intense reaction from the voting public.

Hildy Boespflug, the nurse who testified before the House Judiciary Subcommittee, followed the debate in the legislature from the gallery. She fingered her rosary and held up signs that said, "Oregon, The Suicide State" and "Come to Oregon—Once."[97] Her actions augured the worst fears of those who opposed the Oregon Death with Dignity Act, a decision of the Supreme Court that overturned Judge Hogan's injunction and allowed the Act to go into effect.

Chapter 3

The Law Goes Into Effect:
The Courts Decide

Introduction

One expects rich walnut paneling, an awe-inspiring great seal of the United States, and a judge or judges sitting on a raised dais, when one attends federal court proceedings. One does not anticipate how much civil court proceedings differ from criminal court cases. There is no jury, no cross-examination of witnesses, and no objections by lawyers. Two groups of lawyers submit briefs to the court and then argue on the merits of their case. The judges question them at will and issue a decision at a later time.

The judicial branch relies on evidence and precedents to interpret the law. Contending parties must have suffered harm or loss to bring a case to court. This legal issue, called *standing*, played an important part in several cases that involved the Oregon Death with Dignity Act. Judges sometimes issue contradictory rulings based on the same constitutional or statutory provisions. They have ruled in favor of and against hastened death, citing the same due process clause of the Fourteenth Amendment.

This chapter discusses the court cases that led to the implementation of the Death with Dignity Act. It starts with *Lee v. Oregon* (1994), an appeal to the Ninth Circuit Court, and the decision of that court to withhold its ruling pending the outcome of *Washington v. Glucksberg* (1997). In this last case, the Supreme Court ruled that states could set their own policies on hastened death. The Ninth Circuit Court ordered Hogan's injunction vacated, and the Oregon Death with Dignity Act went into effect.

Table 3.1 Timeline of Court Cases

1994: *Lee v. Oregon*, Judge Hogan declares Oregon Death with Dignity Act unconstitutional.

—*Compassion in Dying v. Washington*

1996: *Lee v. Oregon* appealed to Ninth Circuit Court of Appeals.

—Ninth Circuit Court of Appeals upholds *Compassion in Dying v. Washington*

—Judge Michael Hogan refuses to lift injunction against Oregon's law

1997: *Washington v. Glucksberg*, Ninth Circuit Court of Appeals orders Judge Michael Hogan to vacate his decision in *Lee v. Oregon*.

—Oregon Death with Dignity Act goes into effect

Lee v. Oregon (1994)

A group of physicians, including Dr. Gary Lee and Dr. Bill Petty; several terminally ill patients; and a Catholic nursing home sued to halt the implementation of the Oregon Death with Dignity Act after voters approved it in 1994.[98] They filed suit in a federal district court in Eugene, Oregon, rather than in Portland, Oregon. They hoped to obtain a favorable hearing from Judge Michael R. Hogan, a jurist whose previous decisions had endeared him to social conservatives.[99]

James Bopp, Jr., a well-known right-to-life attorney from Indiana, represented the plaintiffs. He argued that, if the State of Oregon implemented the Act, family members might coerce terminally ill and disabled patients into committing suicide. This constituted a violation of a patient's rights under the First and Fourteenth Amendments, as well as the Americans with Disabilities Act.

Thomas A. Balmer, now an Oregon Supreme Court Judge, represented the State of Oregon. He argued that the citizens of Oregon passed this law through the initiative power reserved them in the Oregon Constitution. Judge Hogan ignored Balmer's argument. He halted implementation of the law on 7 December 1994, the day before it was to take effect.[100]

Coombs Lee accused Hogan of snatching the right to a dignified and peaceful death from the dying at the last minute. Gail Atteberry of Oregon Right to Life disagreed. She believed that the best thing coming out of Hogan's decision was that people now realized the "magnitude" of their vote.[101]

Hogan declared the Death with Dignity Act unconstitutional and issued a permanent injunction preventing implementation on 3 August 1995.[102] He called the Act a "profoundly sloppy piece of work."[103] He stated that it didn't sufficiently differentiate between competent and incompetent patients, establish safeguards in the event of a botched suicide, ensure the competency of attending and consulting physicians, or provide for an independently chosen consulting physician.[104]

Lee v. Oregon in Appellate Court (1996)

Balmer appealed Hogan's decision to the Ninth Circuit Court of Appeals on 9 July 1996. He believed it was an "open and shut case" based on its merits, that is, the right of the citizens of Oregon to pass a law that allowed terminal patients to obtain and take a lethal prescription.[105] Eli Stutsman represented Goodwin, Coombs Lee, and Sinnard, all members of the group that wrote the Oregon Death with Dignity Act. His brief emphasized that the plaintiffs did not have standing because they based their claims on speculation about what might happen to some unknown person at an unidentified time or place.[106]

The judges asked Bopp how Oregon's law had harmed his clients.[107] Bopp insisted there was a likelihood of harm. Balmer and Stutsman agreed beforehand that Balmer would argue the merits of the case and Stutsman would argue the question of standing. When Balmer realized the judges wanted to discuss the issue of standing, he argued that question. He insisted that the danger to Bopp's clients was purely speculative. They would never take advantage of the Act's provisions. The judges of the Ninth Circuit Court delayed their finding until they saw how the Supreme Court ruled on a case involving Compassion in Dying in the states of Washington and New York combined under the title of *Washington v. Glucksberg*.

Compassion in Dying v. Washington (1994)

Several terminal patients filed suit in the federal district court of Western Washington to overturn a Washington State statute criminalizing aiding or assisting a suicide.[108] Other plaintiffs consisted of a group of physicians, including Harold Glucksberg. These physicians believed the Hippocratic oath did not compel them to prolong the act of dying.[109]

Kathryn Tucker, legal counsel for Compassion and Dying, gained experience as legal counsel for the 1991 campaign for initiative 119 in Washington State. She filed a suit for the plaintiffs rather than waiting until the state brought someone to trial for aiding a suicide. She reasoned that if choices central to personal dignity and autonomy include abortion, they also include death by legal lethal prescription.[110] She further argued that the Washington statute interfered with the liberty of competent, terminally ill adults to make end-of-life decisions free of undue government interference.[111]

Judge Barbara J. Rothstein ruled on 3 May 1994 that Washington's law violated the Fourteenth Amendment of the US Constitution, guaranteeing citizens equal protection and due process under the laws of the United States. She noted there was no decision more profound than when a mentally competent adult chose to end their suffering and hasten an inevitable death.[112]

Compassion and Dying v. Washington in Appellate Court (1995)

William L. Williams, Assistant Attorney General of the State of Washington, appealed Rothstein's decision to the Ninth Circuit Court of Appeals. Wesley J. Smith served as amicus curiae (friend of the court) for the International Anti-Euthanasia Task Force. Bopp served as amicus curiae for the National Legal Center for the Medically Dependent and Disabled. Two judges of the Ninth Circuit Court overturned Rothstein's decision on 9 March 1995. They declared there was no constitutional right to commit suicide.

Ninth Circuit Court Reconsiders (1995)

All eleven judges in the Ninth Circuit Court of Appeals voted to reconsider the decision. They heard oral arguments on 26 October 1995.[113] Tucker argued for the plaintiffs. She stated that this case was about whether the government "has the power to intrude into and control this profoundly and uniquely personal decision."[114] Judge Andrew Kleinfeld repeatedly interrupted Tucker, questioning her line of argument. Williams asserted that the statute protected the lives of the poor and minorities from coercion to commit suicide.

Coombs Lee attended the court proceedings in San Francisco. She predicted that Tucker would prevail and a favorable decision would help the Death with Dignity struggle in Oregon. Bopp disagreed. He thought that the judges' intense interest signaled their approval of Williams's arguments.[115]

The full Ninth Circuit Court of Appeals upheld Rothstein's decision by a vote of 8–3 in 1996.[116] They reaffirmed that competent adults with terminal illnesses have a right to die. The majority found that "We are following the constitutional mandate to take such decisions out of the hands of the government" and place them into "the hands of the people."[117]

Judge Stephen Reinhardt predicted that the Court's ruling would precipitate controversy.[118] The editors of the *Oregonian* charged that the decision "contorted the Fourteenth Amendment into a funeral mask."[119] Derek Humphry observed, "By striking down Washington State's prohibition against assisted suicides, the appellate court indirectly approved a law for the dying who express a desire to shorten their suffering with lethal drugs."[120]

As a result of the decision of the Ninth Circuit Court, Balmer and Stutsman petitioned Hogan to lift his injunction against the Oregon Death with Dignity Act. Coombs Lee insisted that if Hogan did not do so, "He ignores the clear instructions of a panel of superior judges."[121] Hogan refused to lift his injunction and joked about "colonial-garbed Dr. Kevorkians proclaiming the new liberty interest from the rooftops."[122]

Washington v. Glucksberg (1997)

On 1 October 1996, the Supreme Court announced it would review *Compassion in Dying v. Washington* and *Quill v. New York*. Sixty-four groups submitted briefs. Bopp authored six briefs and coordinated the effort for several other petitioners, who urged the court to uphold laws in Washington and New York making it a crime to aid or assist a suicide. Briefs from interest groups that represented the disabled argued that the Fourteenth Amendment gives equal protection under the law to the poor, the weak, and the vulnerable.

The American Hospital Association maintained that assisting a patient's death was unethical and incompatible with the Hippocratic imperative that physicians do no harm to a patient.[123] The American Bioethics Committee charged that physician-assisted suicide devalued human life. They cited examples from

Nazi Germany and medical practice in the Netherlands.[124] Church groups claimed that taking another's life was a sin.[125]

Interest groups representing the respondents argued that the Supreme Court should uphold the decisions of two appellate courts. John Rawls, professor of political philosophy at Harvard, stated, "Every competent person has the right to make momentous personal decisions that invoke fundamental religious or philosophical convictions about life's value for himself."[126] Surviving family members contended that the average patient found no difference between refusing life support measures and asking a physician for assistance in hastening death.[127]

Analysts predicted that the Supreme Court would break no new ground by declaring a right to die. However, Balmer believed that any Supreme Court decision would help his appeal of Hogan's decision before the Ninth US Circuit Court. On January 8, 1997, beginning at 10:02 a.m., the Supreme Court heard oral arguments. The justices expressed appreciation at the high quality of the briefs and asked a number of questions.

Williams argued that throughout the history of this country, the states have had an interest in protecting life. Pursuant to this interest, they passed laws against aiding a suicide. In arguing that states had the right to pass such legislation, Williams lent support to Oregon's Death with Dignity Act. He insisted that "our sister state of Oregon may legitimately create an exception to its homicide laws for physician-assisted suicide."[128]

Tucker spoke one sentence. "This case presents the question whether dying citizens in full possession of their mental faculties at the threshold of death due to terminal illness have the liberty to choose to cross that threshold in a humane and dignified manner."[129] Justice William Rehnquist interrupted her in the middle of her next sentence. He stated that the question as he understood it was not an individual's liberty to choose death, but their request for assistance in dying from a physician.

Tucker agreed with Rehnquist. She stated that assistance from a physician was necessary because the dying patients want a peaceful, humane, dignified death. She distinguished protection for those for whom the dying process had begun and those who suffered chronic pain. Justice Anthony Scalia drew laughter with a remark that all of us have begun the dying process.[130]

The Supreme Court issued its ruling on June 6, 1997. One legal observer called it a "victory for the cautious."[131] The majority opinion upheld Washington and New York laws that criminalized aiding a suicide. The justices did not rule on the constitutionality of laws like the Oregon Death with Dignity Act. They left the matter up to the states.

Justice David Souter noted, "Legislatures on the other hand, have superior opportunities to obtain the facts necessary for a judgment about the present controversy."[132] Rehnquist declared, "Americans are engaged in an earnest and profound debate about the morality, legality and practicality of physician-assisted suicide. Our holding permits this debate to continue, as it should in a democratic society."[133]

The Supreme Court didn't resolve the debate.[134] They allowed state courts and legislatures to make these difficult moral and ethical decisions. Conservative legal scholars lauded the *Glucksberg* decision: "The Fourteenth Amendment has not yet become a suicide pact within the Constitution."[135] However, Atteberry of Oregon Right to Life was "absolutely shocked" when she learned that the ruling allowed Oregon's law to go into effect.[136]

Implementation of the Death with Dignity Act (1997)

The Ninth Circuit Court of Appeals ruled that the plaintiffs in *Lee v. Oregon* did not have standing on 27 October 1997.[137] Opponents of Oregon's law appealed, but the US Supreme Court declined to hear the case. The Ninth Circuit Court notified Judge Hogan, who, in turn, dismissed the original complaint on 25 November 1997.[138] Stutsman received notice from Hogan and contacted the Oregon Attorney General's office. That office declared the Death with Dignity Act in force hours before Oregon voters approved the Act for a second time.[139]

Within twenty-four hours of the Attorney General's announcement, state officials prepared forms for prescribing and consulting physicians. Required information included the patient's medical diagnosis and prognosis; the date of the first request for suicide assistance; and an assessment that the patient is capable, fully informed, and acting voluntarily. The patient is informed of alternatives and informed that they can withdraw their request at any time.[140]

The first legal aided death occurred on 24 March 1998. A woman in her mid-nineties with terminal breast cancer died, surrounded by friends and family. In a tape recording of her last comments, she said, "That's all. It's just. I will be relieved of all the stress I have."[141] Opponents of Death with Dignity reacted quickly. Hamilton of Physicians for Compassionate Care charged that physicians assisted her suicide, despite a diagnosis that she was depressed.[142]

Opponents discussed the need of a special session of the Oregon Legislative Assembly to amend the Act to exempt pharmacists who did not wish to prescribe lethal drugs and to establish stricter residency requirements. Senator Neil Bryant (R-Bend) wanted to discuss allowing lethal injection for terminal patients.[143] Right-to-die advocates replied that they never intended that the act include lethal injections. Most legislators believed that they could determine if corrective legislative action was necessary after the State of Oregon implemented the law.

The 1999 legislature approved Senate Bill 491, the result of a collaborative effort among representatives of Providence Health System, Oregon Medical Association, Oregon Health Division, Oregon Pharmacists Association, and Oregon Right to Die. It strengthened residency requirements, exempted pharmacists opposed to writing lethal prescriptions, provided that the estates of persons who chose to die on public property would pay for their burial, stipulated that patients could not avail themselves of the Act based solely on their disability, and allowed Catholic hospitals to discipline physicians who carried out its provisions on hospital property.[144]

Eighmey observed that if the social conservatives had compromised in 1997, they would have secured twenty-two amendments instead of five and avoided defeat in a divisive and expensive election.[145] The real significance of the passage of amendments in 1999 was that people of good faith could compromise, even though they differed on the issue.

Conclusion

Oregonians viewed the Death with Dignity Act as their own. Like most Americans, they agreed with arguments based on opposition to government intrusion into their lives. It did not matter to them if the Attorney General or the lawyers in his department personally believed in the Act. What was important was that the State of Oregon was a party to the case.

Other states considered legislation similar to Oregon's law. In the two years following Glucksberg, eight state legislatures considered bills to legalize hastened death, and eight considered bills to prohibit it. The ensuing debate matched the intensity and fervor of the abortion issue. On a positive note, John Dinan, a political science professor at Wake Forrest, concluded that *Glucksberg* enhanced democratic deliberation, secured representation for competing interests, and provided opportunities for policy experimentation.[146]

The efforts of right-to-life activists to block the Oregon Death with Dignity Act in court ended in failure. The law written by Sinnard and his friends went into effect. However, one election and one court decision was not enough to end a struggle over such high-stakes issues.[147] The resolute opponents of hastened death asked their representatives in Congress to pressure the US Drug Enforcement Administration to punish physicians who prescribed lethal medication and to sponsor legislation that rendered the Act inoperable.[148] At the same time, they prepared for the election called for by the Oregon Legislative Assembly.

Chapter 4

An Expensive and Acrimonious Campaign: The Election of 1997

Introduction

Righteous anger surfaced early in the campaign of 1997. Coombs Lee of Compassion in Dying charged, "The arrogance of the legislature shone bright on the death-with-dignity issue, first by telling voters they didn't understand what they approved in 1994, and then by a blatant attempt to deceive the voters with a misleading ballot title."[149]

The Republicans introduced House Bill 2954 (Ballot Measure 51), a bill that called for a special election on 4 November 1997 to reconsider the Oregon Death with Dignity Act. In addition, they passed House Bill 3502, a bill that allowed them to write the ballot title and explanation instead of the Attorney General. They knew that many citizens used this explanation as their sole source of information on how to cast their vote. Governor Kitzhaber vetoed the bill, because he believed that it circumvented statutory process. He also said that the use of "physician-assisted suicide" instead of the law's actual title, The Death with Dignity Act, reflected the bias of the Republican leadership.

The task of writing the ballot title reverted to Attorney General Hardy Myers (D) after the governor's veto. Myer's ballot summary for Measure 51 read "repeals Measure 16, adopted by voters in 1994. That law: allows terminally ill adult Oregon residents voluntary informed choice to obtain physician's prescription for lethal drugs."[150]

A Debate without Dignity

The 1997 election differed from the 1994 election in several ways. Voters received their ballots by mail. They had three weeks to mail or return them to their county elections department. In addition, only one other measure appeared on the ballot. This meant voters had plenty of time to study the ballot. On the other hand, voters voted "no" on Measure 51 if they wished to retain Measure 16, the Death with Dignity Act. Roger Gafke and David Leuthold cite research in the *Public Opinion Quarterly* that indicates that up to one-third of the electorate votes in error when authors of measures word it in this manner.[151]

Proponents of Measure 51

The Repeal Measure 16 Committee hired Chuck Cavalier and Associates, the director of the successful campaign against Proposition 161 in California in 1992, to manage the campaign against the Death with Dignity Act. Cavalier urged Physicians for Compassionate Care, a group of physicians and health care professionals, to take the leading role in the campaign.[152] He asked the Church to lower its profile and play down the religious arguments it used in the 1994 campaign. Kenneth Steiner, Auxiliary Bishop of Portland, concurred, "We didn't want this to backfire on us as it did in 1994."[153]

Steiner formed alliances with churches and groups who supported repeal of Measure 16, including the Church of Jesus Christ of Latter-Day Saints. Pastors in parishes and bishops in stakes read letters condemning assisted suicide. Several Evangelical Protestant churches took similar stands. The Oregon Hospice Association and the Oregon State Council for Senior Citizens joined the coalition. Members of Physicians for Compassionate Care waged a successful campaign to change the position of the Oregon Medical Association from neutrality to one of support for repeal of the Death with Dignity Act.

The Repeal Measure 16 Committee collected $3.8 million in contributions. The largest single contribution, $400,000, came from Oregon Right to Life. Several Catholic institutions contributed a total of $600,000.[154] These funds financed rallies, panels of physicians, phone banks, billboards, media ads, and mailings. Every bit of advertising, including 100,000 lawn signs, repeated the theme: "Fatally Flawed."

Physicians for Compassionate Care portrayed the Death with Dignity Act as "terrible social policy wrapped in a slick rhetorical package."[155] Members spoke in local forums and from pulpits. They insisted that oral medications caused horrific deaths, charged that physicians often misdiagnosed terminal illnesses, and feared inadequate screening procedures would not detect those who wished to end their lives because of depression.

Opponents of Measure 51

The Oregon Right to Die Committee spent $966,000. George Soros, the international financier, gave $25,000. The largest organizational contribution, $74,000, came from the Hemlock Society.[156] The remainder of the contributions came in small amounts from individual donors from all over the country. The committee could not afford television advertising until the last month of the campaign. Faye Girsh, executive director of the Hemlock Society, noted, "We don't have pulpits. We don't have congregations. We don't have fire and brimstone."[157]

The Oregon Right to Die Committee commissioned a poll that indicated that 80 percent of the respondents strongly agreed that the legislature should never return a measure previously approved by the voters. Derek Humphry predicted that the public would turn against the legislature, and he forecast a runaway victory for supporters of the Death with Dignity Act. Twenty-two newspapers wrote forty-three editorials against referral.[158]

The Campaign

Oregon Right to Die employed two successful tactics in 1994—heartrending stories and resentment over the involvement of the Catholic Church. They told voters about Peggy Satchell, a sixty-three-year-old who wanted the right to seek her doctor's aid in dying. Satchell resented the intense lobbying of the legislature by Oregon Right to Life and the Catholic Conference.[159] A caller to a radio talk show charged that the Church, as a foreign power, could not legally contribute to the campaign. [160]

The "Don't Let 'Em Shove Their Religion Down Your Throat Committee" sponsored a radio ad that accused politicians in the state legislature and the Catholic Church of making statements based on distorted evidence.[161] Bishop Steiner lamented this "blatantly discriminatory" ad directed at the Catholic Church.[162] Coombs Lee argued that the Catholic Church brought in "millions of dollars to essentially make the Oregon government enforce its doctrine."[163] She insisted that she had no quarrel with the Catholic religion, only its hierarchy.[164]

One Oregon Right to Die television commercial featured testimony from Dorothy Hoogstraat about her husband's death. She claimed politicians condemned him to an agonizing death when they took away his opportunity to obtain a legal lethal prescription. She noted that a great deal of the money for repeal came from the Catholic Church, an organization that wished to impose its views on the rest of society. In the last frame, the narrator argued for choice in end-of-life decisions.[165]

Another Right to Die television ad featured Sinnard, one of the founders of Oregon Death with Dignity. He criticized the legislature for referring the Death with Dignity Act back to the voters at the behest of the Catholic Church and conservative political organizations. Polling by the Right to Die Committee indicated that people rated this commercial poorly in comparison to the others, so they rarely aired it.[166]

Right-to-life advocates counterattacked with several new commercials. One featured a bottle of pills. Various images flashed on the surface of the bottle. First, the word "poison," then a skull and crossbones, and finally the face of an agonized woman appeared on the bottle. In closing the announcer declared, "The pills don't work 25 percent of the time."[167] The advertisement characterized the Death with Dignity Act as fatally flawed legislation that would kill people.

Coombs Lee retorted, "It's fatally flawed that we have to vote on this again."[168] She accused opponents of creating a "well-orchestrated conspiracy of lies." She produced a letter from Dutch physician Pieter Admiraal that stated the failure rate for hastened death by oral medication cited by opponents of the measure distorted his research.[169] She insisted that lethal oral medications were humane and effective.

Several television outlets refused to air an ad entitled "Billy." It showed a young man in apparent good health contemplating suicide. Right-to-die activists labeled this ad a scare tactic, because the Death with Dignity Act applied only to terminally ill patients with less than six months to live. Coombs Lee noted, "When they hired Chuck Cavalier, we expected it. His method is to find something scary and buy a lot of TV time."[170]

The *Catholic Sentinel* and the *Oregonian* endorsed Measure 51 to repeal the Death with Dignity Act, the only two newspapers in Oregon to do so. Assistant editor David Reinhard penned a series of editorials in the *Oregonian*, titled "Liar,

Liar." He accused Death with Dignity supporters of flirting with bigotry and described their commercials as "flatly fraudulent."[171]

David Smigelski, of *Willamette Week*, reported that the studies quoted by Reinhard had nothing to do with hastened death.[172] He accused the editors and writers of the *Oregonian* of taking sides in the election. Coombs Lee echoed these charges. She particularly objected to a cartoon that appeared on the editorial page that depicted a physician holding a hangman's noose.[173] A series of letters to the editors reinforced her point. Shendy McAtee wrote, "One word—biased—describes your editorials on Measure 51."[174]

The Voters' Pamphlet

The arguments of the Repeal Measure 16 Committee in the Voters' Pamphlet stayed on message. The Oregon Legislature explained that they submitted the measure to the voters because it lacked adequate safeguards, and new information indicated that the drugs used in hastening death were not effective. Twenty-six individuals and groups paid $300 to include their arguments for repeal. The Catholic clergy did not submit a statement.[175]

The Voters' Pamphlet contained sixteen arguments opposing the repeal of the Death with Dignity Act. Coombs Lee urged voters not to let the legislature take away their vote. Arguments submitted by physicians, pharmacists, and other health care professionals countered arguments made by their professional peers favoring repeal of the law. Penny Schleuter, the woman who testified before the House Judiciary Committee, asked voters not to impose their wishes on those who had different values and beliefs.[176]

The Vote

Oregon voters chose to retain the Death with Dignity Act on 4 November 1997. The count was 666,275 for retention, and 445,830 for repeal.[177] A jubilant Coombs Lee announced the defeat of Measure 51. "Oregon voters didn't just say 'no.' They said, 'Hell no!'"[178] She declared that the people of Oregon had spoken twice at the ballot box and that it was time for the law to take effect.[179] Castagna, spokesperson for the Oregon Catholic Conference, labeled it "a tragic day for Oregon, the nation and the world."[180]

There are no exit polls in a mail-in election, but available evidence indicated that voters had already made up their minds on the issue well in advance of the election.[181] Bill Lunch, a political science professor at Oregon State University, observed that voters decided during the first election in 1994.[182] Voters returned their ballots early, a sign that they knew how they wanted to vote.

Urban liberal counties and precincts with a large number of elderly people voted overwhelmingly to retain the Death with Dignity Act. One coastal precinct, the location of several large retirement homes, supported the law by a 79 percent margin.[183] A survey by Adam Davis and Tim Hibbitts indicated that most of those favoring repeal were registered Republicans who attended church regularly. Those favoring retention showed higher levels of education, were members of the Democratic Party, and not affiliated with a church or synagogue.[184]

Age proved a significant factor in determining support of the Oregon Death with Dignity Act. Some seniors thought the Act ensured that their families honored their end-of-life choices. Others believed in their right of personal autonomy. A college professor told the story of his eighty-year-old father, who turned off his hearing aid during sermons and voted to retain the act, even though his priest said it was a sin.

Langlois of the *Catholic Sentinel* reported that a survey commissioned by the National Conference of Catholic Bishops indicated that end-of-life decisions came not from political advertising, but from personal introspection.[185] Most people (45 percent) talked to friends and family. Another 35 percent reported newspapers helped them decide. Respondents cited the church (25 percent) and television ads (23 percent) as additional sources of information. The survey indicated that Catholics who attended services weekly were more likely to support the church's position on assisted suicide than Catholics who attended less often.[186]

Conclusion

Proponents of Death with Dignity argued that support of the Act was not confined to one political party. Many Republicans expressed a strong belief in the rights of the individual.[187] Dr. Peter Goodwin, who helped write Oregon's Death with Dignity Act, argued that more and more people recognized the issue as one of personal freedom.[188] Nicholas van Aelstyn, counsel for the Compassion in Dying Federation, observed that although some viewed the right to die as a liberal issue, for most people it was a libertarian issue.[189]

However, most political analysts believed that the significant factor in the vote was anger at the legislature's decision to refer the Act back to the people. One irate citizen charged the legislature with assuming the role of a chiding parent in a letter to the editor.[190] A headline in the *Catholic Sentinel* proclaimed, "Pro-Euthanasia Oregon Voters Driven by Anger at Legislature."[191] Others argued that Oregonians thought of themselves as mavericks accustomed to passing groundbreaking legislation. Steve Duin of the *Oregonian*, in an article titled "Votin', Gloatin' Pioneers," contended that money and lobbyists deluded the voters.[192]

Ellen Goodman, the syndicated columnist, observed, "Step by careful step, the rest of us have begun to follow the Oregon Trail."[193] Marla Rothouse, a policy specialist for the National Conference of State Legislatures, did not think that other states would follow Oregon's lead, but predicted that Oregon's vote would encourage other states to deal more aggressively with palliative care.[194] Opponents of Death with Dignity argue with this conclusion, but this much is sure, the contentious debate continued.

One right-to-die advocate asked the foes of the law to stop trying to defeat the Death with Dignity Act because, "They had a chance to vote."[195] The persistent foes of the Act disagreed. Hamilton of Physicians for Compassionate Care observed that the debate was far from over.[196]

Professor Thomas W. Mayo, a professor of law at Texas Christian University, believes that the discussions over life and death issues are necessary for a healthy democracy. He described the process as "a never-ending conversation among citizens and the nation's three branches of government."[197]

Opponents of the Oregon Death with Dignity Act halted implementation of the act after it first passed in 1994. The battle over the Act played out in legal, legislative, and initiative campaigns. The tone of the argument in the courts was more subtle and rarified than the emotional rhetoric of the legislature and the clamor of the referendum. The resolute and resourceful opponents of Death with Dignity sought relief from these defeats in the Congress of the United States; armed with a foreknowledge of a favorable reception from the Republican majority, a modicum of legislative acumen, their faith-based rhetoric, and hopes of victory.

Part II. Keeping What You Got:

Recurring Maintenance

Chapters 5–7

Chapter 5

Solace for Whom? Death with Dignity in Congress

Introduction

Pat Matheny, a forty-five-year-old cabinetmaker from Coos Bay, Oregon, suffered from amyotrophic lateral sclerosis (ALS). Matheny recalled an agreement he made with his brother. "We made a deal when we were young that if any one of us became a vegetable, the other one had to do ya."[198] A Hemlock Society volunteer put Matheny in contact with a patient advocate at the Oregon Health & Science University. The advocate found two physicians who agreed that Matheny had six months to live. Matheny requested and received a lethal prescription from a prescribing physician. Matheny died on 10 March 1999.[199] His brother-in-law held the glass while Matheny ingested a mixture of nutrition drink and barbiturates.

N. Greg Hamilton of Physicians for Compassionate Care accused Matheny's brother-in-law of murder, because the Oregon Death with Dignity Act requires patients to ingest the medication by themselves.[200] After investigating the case, the Coos Bay district attorney refused to press charges. Hamilton viewed Matheny's difficulty swallowing as a basis to assert that someone might use the Americans with Disabilities Act to demand a lethal injection.[201] Outraged by what they saw as abuses of the law, other opponents asked the Drug Enforcement Agency (DEA) and a Republican-controlled Congress for help.

They requested a ruling on using controlled substances to legally hasten death from Thomas Constantine, the administrator of the DEA. He advised Representative Henry Hyde (R-IL) that Oregon's law violated the Controlled Substances Act (CSA).[202] Attorney General Janet Reno overruled Constantine on 5 June 1998. She wrote to Hyde that the Death with Dignity Act didn't

41

violate the Controlled Substances Act because the State of Oregon had the authority to determine legitimate medical practice within its borders.[203]

105th Congress, 1997–1999

Senator Ron Wyden (D-OR) voted twice against the Death with Dignity Act as an Oregon voter.[204] He did not think the Act provided enough protection for senior citizens. He conceded his fears were unfounded, because the Act's safeguards worked quite well in preventing abuses.[205] If given the opportunity to vote on the issue again, he didn't know how he would vote. Wyden believed that his obligation to defend the decisions of his constituents at the ballot box outweighed his personal beliefs. He brought considerable determination and experience as a member of Congress in defense of Oregon's Death with Dignity law.

House of Representatives

Hyde introduced the Lethal Drug Abuse and Prevention Act (HR 4006) into the House the day he received Reno's letter. This bill called for a medical review board that had the power to revoke the federal drug-prescribing privileges of physicians who prescribed lethal drugs under Oregon's law and gave the attorney general authority to subpoena reports from the Oregon Department of Health Services to identify physicians who did so.[206]

Compassion in Dying lobbyists formed The National Pain Care Coalition, composed of hospice, medical, and right-to-die groups to oppose the bill. They convinced the American Medical Association and the National Hospice Organization that the bill was detrimental to end-of-life care. Representative Greg Ganske (R-IA), a renegade pro-life physician, wrote a letter to his colleagues in which he noted "fear of investigation will lead to less appropriate pain care and could have the unintended result of increasing the demand for assisted-suicide."[207]

Governor Kitzhaber testified during hearings that if physicians feared investigation by a federal drug agent, they would not treat pain as aggressively as they should. Hyde observed that, although he would not compare Oregon's law with Nazi Germany, the devaluation of human life could lead to similar consequences. He observed, "Why not just suffocate them? Why not use a pillow?"[208]

The Judiciary Committee passed the bill after two and a half hours of debate. Barney Frank (D-MA) argued that the bill told the people of Oregon,

"You are wrong, you cannot make these choices."[209] Hyde retorted, "Innocent human life is not subject to referenda."[210] The impeachment of President Bill Clinton (D) soon absorbed all of Hyde's time, forcing opponents of Oregon's law to shift their efforts to the Senate.[211]

Senate

Senator Don Nickles (R-OK) inserted a one-sentence amendment in an appropriations bill that blocked implementation of Oregon's Death with Dignity Act. The Clinton administration opposed this move. Wyden promised to filibuster any bill so amended. Nickles introduced Representative Hyde's Lethal Drug Abuse and Prevention Act into the Senate. Wyden insisted Congress was wrong if it overrode what the voters of Oregon had decided in two different elections. He asserted that doing so would intensify the public's growing frustration and cynicism with government.[212]

Senator Orin Hatch (R-UT) asked the Clinton administration for input on the Lethal Drug Abuse and Prevention Act when it reached the Judiciary Committee. A spokesperson from the Justice Department wrote that, although President Clinton opposed assisted suicide, the president believed that Nickles's bill would detract from the DEA's primary mission of preventing illegal drug abuse.

The Judiciary Committee approved three amendments to the bill. The first required clear and convincing evidence that physicians intended death, rather than pain relief. The second established a medical review board that included members from the US Department of Human Services to investigate charges against physicians. The third forbade prosecution of physicians who prescribed legal lethal drugs before the approval of the bill.

The Judiciary Committee approved the bill as amended and sent it to the floor of the Senate.[213] Hatch argued that the bill had a better chance of passing in the next session of Congress.[214] Nickles persisted. He tried to add the provisions of the Lethal Drug Abuse and Prevention bill to an appropriations bill. Wyden reminded Republicans of Clinton's promise to veto any appropriations bill festooned with riders.[215] Nickles finally gave in, but promised to introduce similar legislation in the next session.[216]

Right-to-die supporters felt relief that they survived the challenges of the 105th Congress.[217] Coombs Lee credited The National Pain Care Coalition and Senator Wyden with successfully defending the Death with Dignity Act. She believed this was a major accomplishment, considering the power of right-to-life groups.[218]

Richard Doerflinger, of the National Council of Bishops, said, "There are just too many forces conspiring against it at this point."[219] Disputed deaths like Matheny's intensified opponents' desire to overturn the Act or prevent its operation. They promised to try again in the next session of Congress. Meanwhile, another death occurred that convinced opponents of the Death with Dignity Act that they were correct in their assessment that it was fatally flawed.

Kate Cheney Asks to Die

Cheney, an eighty-five-year-old Portland woman, decided to hasten her death after she learned that she had stomach cancer and had less than six months to live. She requested a lethal prescription from her doctor at Kaiser Permanente. Her physician refused, so she asked another physician, who arranged for a psychiatric evaluation. A psychologist reported that Cheney understood that she had a short time to live, but couldn't remember the name of her new doctor. Cheney's daughter Erika helped her formulate her answers during the examination. The psychiatrist denied the prescription, because he believed that Erika coerced her mother into asking for it.

Cheney asked for a second evaluation. A clinical psychologist declared her competent, even though her daughter was "somewhat coercive."[220] Faced with conflicting opinions, Cheney's physician met with Dr. Robert Richardson, director of the Kaiser Permanente Northwest Ethics Service. After talking to Cheney, Richardson concluded that she was acting on her own and should receive the prescription.

Cheney received the drugs on July 23, 1999. She announced, "I'm going to meet my husband again and meet my father again."[221] The next month she called her friends on the phone, met with her family for a toast of Liebfraumilch wine, and ingested a mixture of applesauce and lethal drugs. She died peacefully within an hour.

Newspaper stories on her death generated another round of controversy. Hamilton accused Kaiser Permanente of giving an elderly Oregon woman with dementia a lethal overdose of federally controlled substances, despite the fact that a psychiatrist had found she was not eligible for assisted suicide.[222] He concluded, "Once assisted suicide is legalized, there is no way to protect the vulnerable and mentally ill."[223]

Richardson replied to these attacks in an e-mail to the *Oregonian*. He expressed sorrow that Kate's family and her caregivers "were subjected to this mean-spirited, misinformed and undeserved attack."[224] Columnist Steve Duin observed, "A measure of its compassion is that Kate Cheney—now in the company of a loving God—is no longer around to hear how painfully others twisted her story to fit a variety of agendas."[225] Reinhard of the *Oregonian* repeated these allegations in an editorial titled "In the Dark Shadows of Measure 16." Opponents of the Death with Dignity Act included their version of the Cheney story in testimony during the next session of Congress.

106th Congress, 1999–2001

Hyde introduced the Pain Relief Promotion Act (HR 2260) into the House in 1999. Its title mentions pain relief, a difference in emphasis from the Lethal Drug Abuse and Prevention Act. It authorized $5 million to teach physicians pain management techniques. The National Hospice Association and the American Medical Association changed their position and supported the bill as a result of this change.

Compassion in Dying of Oregon disagreed. "This bill is not intended to relieve pain—it is solely intended to overturn Oregon's law."[226] The bill provided the Justice Department $80 million to investigate Oregon physicians who used controlled substances to legally hasten the death of terminal patients.[227] Ann Jackson, director of the Oregon Hospice Association, observed, "It's really scary. Oregon is going to be hung out to dry."[228]

House of Representatives

Senator Hyde lambasted physicians who carried out the provisions of Oregon's law as "hangmen" and "messengers of death."[229] Governor Kitzhaber testified against the bill, to no avail. The bill passed the House 271–156. Representative Bart Stupak (D-MI) remarked, "I bet you if this becomes a law, I'm sure Oregon will be able to come up with some concoction that's not using federally controlled substances to implement their assisted suicide."[230]

Senate

Wyden called a news conference on the steps of the Capitol when he learned that Senator Hatch, chairman of the House Judiciary Committee, did not intend to hold hearings on the Pain Relief Promotion Act. He observed, "This is about throwing the law of a small state, located many miles from the capital into the trashcan because it does not comport with the personal and religious beliefs of some in Washington D.C."[231] Wyden's rhetoric proved effective. Hatch grudgingly scheduled hearings on 25 April 2000.

Wyden chided the fair-weather friends of states' rights during the hearings. He added, "I firmly believe that my election certificate does not give me the authority to substitute my personal and religious beliefs for the judgment made twice by the people of Oregon."[232]

Senator Gordon Smith (R-OR) declared that his conscience dictated that he support legislation blocking Oregon's Death with Dignity Act. He insisted, "I cannot abide physicians whipping up a poisonous pudding and feeding it to dying people."[233] Duin, in a column in the *Oregonian* titled "His Conscience Provides Solace Only for One," offered Smith this advice: "The dying need to wrestle with their conscience, not yours."[234]

The Judiciary Committee passed the Pain Relief Promotion Act by a 10-to-8 margin on 27 April 2000. Senator Joe Biden (D-DE) voted with the majority. Wyden's staff prepared a cart filled with literature on the Death with Dignity Act for him to read during a filibuster in the event the bill reached the floor of the Senate.[235] Nickles thought he might have the forty votes needed to force cloture. However, Wyden had support among prominent Democrats like Daniel Patrick Moynihan (NY) and Republican states' rights senators, and time was running out in the session.[236] Nickles tried another tactic. He threatened to block a timber appropriation bill, The Secure Rural Schools and Community Self-Determination Act, coauthored by Wyden, unless Wyden agreed to forego filibustering.

The Wyden timber bill added $170 million a year in payments to counties with federal forests, most of which were in Oregon. Senator Smith observed, "This is hardball politics."[237] A headline in the *Oregonian* warned "Don't Bully Oregon."[238] Wyden and Nickles compromised. Nickles would find another way to pass the Pain Relief Promotion Act, and Wyden agreed to stop threatening a filibuster. Nickles relented, and the Senate passed the timber appropriation bill.

Majority Leader Trent Lott (R-MS) announced a few days later that "he planned to offer Nickles's bill as an amendment to an annual spending bill."[239] Wyden reiterated his contention that the President would veto any bill with extraneous riders. Lott bowed to pressure from the White House and chose not to amend the spending bill.

Nickles asked House Majority Leader Dick Armey (R-TX) to include the Pain Relief Act in a tax bill.[240] This legislation passed the House. When it reached the Senate, Majority Leader Trent Lott (R-MS) brought Nickles and Wyden together in hopes of avoiding a filibuster. Wyden insisted that Nickles's amendment would hinder a doctor's ability to treat dying patients. Nickles fumed, "Hogwash."[241] He argued that if Oklahomans passed a referendum that legalized heroin, "It doesn't make it legal. It's still against the law to use heroin."[242]

Minority Leader Tom Daschle (D-SD) declared, "I come to the floor chagrined, disappointed, angered, frustrated."[243] He excoriated Republicans for slipping a controversial amendment into a tax bill at the last minute. He reminded them that Clinton promised that he would not veto the tax bill solely because pain relief legislation was attached to it. He would, however, veto the bill because it had other objectionable amendments, especially one that authorized excessive payments to health maintenance organizations.

The threat of a veto brought back bitter memories of the disaster of shutting down the government in 1996. Lott removed the offending amendment from the tax bill, thus ensuring the President's signature. Wyden announced victory.[244] He promised, "Should Nickles continue to use the United States Senate to overturn the will of the people of Oregon, I will not back down."[245] Nickles vowed to try again in the future. Presidential candidate G. W. Bush (R), in a campaign visit to Oregon, promised that he would sign a similar bill once he became president.[246]

Conclusion

Pressure from the National Pain Coalition, Wyden's quick response to possible amendments, and Congress's desire for adjournment played a part in the defeat of the Lethal Drug Abuse and Prevention Act in the 105th Congress. Wyden's coalition of one blocked passage of the Pain Prevention Act in the 106th Congress.[247] The Newsletter of the Compassion in Dying Federation praised him for his "diligence and dedication."[248]

The people of Oregon reacted negatively to Congress's interference. They expressed strong support for what they felt was their law. Ronald E. Nelson, owner of a Portland, Oregon, dance studio, stated: "The people of Oregon had a vote. I may not agree with it, but is Congress really saying that our vote doesn't count, it doesn't matter? That's just wrong."[249]

Both sides demonstrated resourcefulness and indefatigable determination during the struggle in Congress. Proponents repeated emotional stories of people dying in pain, arguments about the importance of personal choice, and states' rights. Matheny and Cheney explained the reasons for their choices and expressed appreciation to the voters of Oregon for passing the Act.

Opponents commented on the deaths of Cheney and Matheny. They used the slippery slope argument—that these cases typified the threats to the lives of the poor, the aged, and the infirm that were to come. Hamilton's charges appeared in a chapter in Drs. Foley and Hendin's work, *The Case Against Assisted Suicide*, titled "Oregon's Culture of Silence," scholarly journals, friend of the court briefs, and testimony before the House of Lords in the United Kingdom.

Senator Smith accurately described the struggle in both sessions as hardball politics. The parliamentary maneuvering, amendments, threats, and harsh rhetoric employed by both sides were indicative that this was a major battle in the culture war. As a result of the debate over abortion, right-to-life advocates enjoyed well-organized forces at the local, state, and national levels. They promised to use these forces to support candidates who opposed Oregon's law.

The discourse continued unabated. Individual autonomy is a widely shared value among physicians and the public. Attitudes are changing, one voter at a time. Even so, the outcome of the contest is difficult to predict. This much is certain: the debate forced the nation to address problems of pain management and care at the end-of-life. The Act's resolute foes will continue their attack on Oregon's controversial law.

Wyden stated that Nickles would not continue his efforts in the 107th Congress. He predicted that it seemed "more likely that President-elect Bush will simply instruct his Attorney General to reinterpret federal law" to render the Death with Dignity Act inoperable.[250] Wyden's prediction proved accurate. On 6 November 2001, Attorney General John Ashcroft issued a memorandum that prohibited physicians from using controlled substances to legally hasten death and sanctioned those who did so.

Chapter 6

Separating Death from Agony: *Oregon v. Ashcroft* (2001)

Introduction

The people of Medford, a city of 70,000 in Southern Oregon, experienced the impact of the Oregon Death with Dignity Act firsthand when Joan Lucas, a respected member of their community, hastened her death on 3 February 2000. Lucas suffered from amyotrophic lateral sclerosis (ALS). She had no feeling on her right side, had difficulty speaking, and used a computer to communicate. Her formal request for a legal lethal prescription read, "This is to assure you that I wish to end my life by taking a lethal drug. I don't have time to waste."[251]

A counselor from Oregon Death and Dying, a right-to-die group, along with a registered nurse, visited Lucas on the day she chose to die. They asked her if she still wished to swallow the prescription. She replied, "I'm ready" and said good-bye to her family.[252] The women stayed with her and the men went outside to talk. She took the prescription, lost consciousness in five minutes, and died peacefully within an hour.

Lucas's family was not prepared for the controversy that resulted from newspaper articles about their mother's death. The editors of the *Mail Tribune* commented, "Joan Lucas lived a life filled with love and laughter. She chose to end it when it became far less. Oregon voters were right to give her that choice."[253] Dr. N. Greg Hamilton, spokesperson for Physicians for Compassionate Care, called the physician who wrote the prescription a "suicide doctor." He argued that the Oregon Death with Dignity Act was a "tragic failure" because it didn't protect the depressed.[254]

This chapter describes how opponents of Oregon's law successfully appealed to the executive branch of the federal government to sanction physicians who prescribed legal lethal drugs for their patients and the subsequent legal battle by proponents to overturn this directive. It follows *Oregon v. Ashcroft* from its beginnings as a memorandum from Attorney General John Ashcroft, to Federal District Court, and an appeal to the Ninth Circuit Court of Appeals.

Table 6.1 Timeline of Executive and Judicial Events[255]

6 November 2001	- Ashcroft issues directive
23 Sep. 2002	- Ashcroft appeals to Ninth Circuit Court
26 May 2004	- Ninth US Circuit Court rules in favor of Oregon
1 August 2004	- Ninth US Circuit Court denies Ashcroft request for a rehearing
26 February 2005	- US Supreme Court agrees to hear the case

A Smattering of Rumors

Opponents of Death with Dignity expected President G. W. Bush to overturn or invalidate Oregon's law. They urged the President to issue an executive order to Attorney General John Ashcroft to overturn Reno's decision on controlled substances. Hardy Myers, Oregon's Attorney General, wrote to Ashcroft, asking him to notify the State of Oregon of any proposed policy changes.

Castagna, of the Oregon Catholic Conference, worried about the length of time it took for the Justice Department to act. He believed a Supreme Court ruling that federal law superseded a California medical marijuana statute also supported a challenge to the Death with Dignity Act. Garett Epps, a University of Oregon law professor, counter-argued that the Supreme Court would find hastened death a more intimate and personal issue. He observed that the judges had probably not smoked marijuana, but most likely had considered their own deaths.[256]

Josh Kardon, Wyden's chief of staff, claimed that the Justice Department surreptitiously discussed a ruling on the applicability of the Controlled Sub-

stances Act (CSA). He warned that some extremely disciplined political opera-
tives ran the Bush administration, "So whatever they do, they will have a political reason, and they'll do it with great precision."[257] David O'Steen, executive
director of the National Right to Life Committee, argued the contrary—that if
the Justice Department discussed the matter, they would base their conclusions
on law.[258] President Bush refused to meet with Representative Darlene Hooley
(D-OR) to discuss these rumors.[259]

Rumors became reality on 6 November 2001. Ashcroft issued a drug
enforcement policy that blocked the Oregon Death with Dignity law. He
distinguished between hastening a patient's death and the use of controlled
substances to manage pain. He prohibited physicians from prescribing lethal
doses of federally controlled drugs to terminally ill patients and threatened
to revoke the licenses of these prescribing physicians.[260] Ashcroft insisted
that he had the authority to obtain the dispensing record filed with the Oregon Department of Human Services (DHS) to investigate the actions of
physicians.[261]

This policy went into effect only after it was published in the federal register. It specifically exempted from sanctions physicians who prescribed legal
lethal drugs before Ashcroft issued the directive. Reactions to Ashcroft's memorandum came quickly. Oregon Attorney General Hardy Myers and Coombs
Lee of the Compassion in Dying Federation announced plans for a challenge in
federal court to Ashcroft's directive.[262]

Atteberry, director of Oregon Right to Life, expressed her happiness with
Ashcroft's decision. "We commend Attorney General Ashcroft for ending this
outrageous use of drugs."[263] Hamilton expressed relief at the return of Oregon
to the other forty-nine states.[264] On the other hand, the editors of the *St. Petersburg Times* described Ashcroft's memorandum as a part of the culture war.[265]
Ellen Goodman, in a column titled "Ashcroft's Assisted Suicide Stance Is Simply Bizarre," observed, "Let me see if I have this straight. We have terrorists on
the loose, anthrax wafting through the mail, and the Justice Department is in
hot pursuit of terminally ill patients?"[266]

People who wished to legally hasten their deaths hurried to get their lethal
prescriptions filled before physicians stopped writing them.[267] One patient
threatened to shoot himself if the courts did not uphold Oregon's law. Eighmey
responded to suggestions that physicians could prescribe substances not con-

trolled by the federal drug administration. "There are no humane and dignified ways to die without federally controlled substances."[268]

Oregon Challenges The Ashcroft Memorandum

On 7 November 2001, Myers, oncologist Dr. Peter Rasmussen, pharmacist David M. Hochhalter, and four terminally ill patients—Richard Holmes, Karl Stansell, Jane Doe #1, and James Romney—filed a motion in Federal District Court seeking a temporary injunction preventing the federal government from implementing Ashcroft's directive. Myers challenged Ashcroft's authority to limit the practice of medicine in Oregon. He asserted that Ashcroft exceeded the authority delegated to him by Congress to enforce the CSA.[269]

The stories of two of the plaintiffs, Holmes and Romney, illustrate an important aspect of the Oregon Death with Dignity Act. Both men had six months or less to live, received lethal prescriptions under the Act, and died without taking them.[270] Holmes, a frank and engaging retired sales person, died in the arms of his son on 9 September 2002 from complications due to colon and liver cancer at the age of seventy-two years.[271] Although Holmes attended the University of Portland, a Catholic institution, he did not identify with any denomination. He observed, "I lived my life the way I want to. I should die the way I want to."[272]

Romney dedicated his life to the education of young people and enjoyed his work as a high school principal. He died at fifty-seven years of age on 13 May 2003, due to a pulmonary embolism while in the hospital to undergo insertion of a feeding tube. Romney was a member of the Church of Jesus Christ of Latter-Day Saints. He considered religion an important part of his life but wanted "control over when I die because the symptoms of ALS make dying with dignity difficult."[273]

US District Court Judge Robert E. Jones granted a temporary restraining order against Ashcroft's directive on 9 November 2001. The following day Jones stated that he intended it to preserve the status quo until he could hear arguments from both sides. Jones believed that this was fair since several of the plaintiffs hovered close to death and the US government had taken a long time to issue the memorandum.[274]

Preliminary Hearing

Jones heard four hours of testimony in the case of *Oregon v. Ashcroft* on Tuesday, 20 November 2001. Steve Bushong, assistant attorney general of Oregon, acted as the lead attorney for the plaintiffs, seconded by Eli Stutsman, Nicholas van Aelstyn, and Kathryn Tucker. Assistant US Attorney Craig Casey served as the lead attorney for the defense, seconded by William Howard and George Katsas of the Justice Department.

Jones set the ground rules for the hearing and asked the attorneys from both sides to introduce themselves. Bushong spoke first for the State of Oregon. Minutes into his argument, Jones asked him if he wasn't ignoring whether Attorney General Ashcroft issued his directive in violation of the Administrative Procedures Act, a law that allowed for public comment.[275] Bushong took the hint, departed from his prepared remarks, and lambasted the secrecy of the US Attorney General.[276]

The judge peppered attorneys from both sides with questions. Katsas, representing the federal government, repeatedly mispronounced the word "Oregon." Jones commented in a humorous vein, "Now, you just committed an original sin. (Laughter) It is 'Oregon' enunciating, 'Or-e-gun.' (Laughter.) Now with that behind you, collect your thoughts and start over."[277] Katsas recovered and argued that Ashcroft's decision reinterpreted an old policy, and therefore the provisions of the Administrative Procedures Act did not apply.

Jones issued a temporary injunction pending his final decision. He declared Ashcroft's directive unenforceable and of no legal effect. He exempted physicians, pharmacists, and healthcare providers who complied with the Oregon Death with Dignity Act from criminal prosecution or other administrative procedures.[278] Jones asked permission to expedite the case, because several of the plaintiffs might not live long enough to learn its outcome.

Both sides responded immediately. Ed Langlois, a reporter for the *Catholic Sentinel*, stated that Oregonians could still "snuff life."[279] Plaintiff Richard Holmes noted, "It means I can get my prescription. It's a great victory for the people of Oregon."[280]

Final Hearing

Jones held a three-hour hearing on 21 March 2002. The plaintiffs targeted Ashcroft's alleged violation of the Administrative Procedures Act and his authority under the CSA. The attorneys for the US Department of Justice answered that federal law required plaintiffs to challenge policy decisions of the executive branch in the Ninth Federal Appellate Court and that the plaintiffs brought their case to the wrong court. Jones ruled that his court had jurisdiction and that he would decide the case on procedural rather than constitutional issues. He promised to announce his decision between April 17 and 19, 2002.

On Wednesday, 17 April 2002, Jones declared that the US Justice Department did not have the authority to interfere with medical practice in Oregon, that Ashcroft exceeded his authority under the Controlled Substances Act, and stifled debate on the issue.[281] He issued a permanent injunction that exempted physicians, pharmacists, and other healthcare providers from criminal prosecution or other administrative actions.[282]

US Attorney Robert McCallum remarked, "We're disappointed with Judge Jones's ruling."[283] McCallum promised to take the case to the Appeals Court and, if necessary, the Supreme Court. Stephen Gold, representing Not Dead Yet, an interest group of disabled activists, forecast that given the makeup and ideology of the Supreme Court, its opposition to assisted suicide would prevail over states' rights.[284]

The Ninth Federal Circuit Court of Appeals

Ashcroft appealed Jones's decision to the Ninth Federal Circuit Court of Appeals on 23 September 2002. He reiterated his conviction that "Suicide is not a legitimate medical purpose."[285] Hamilton noted in his brief that the federal government should regulate the practice of medicine by requiring that states uniformly apply laws concerning federally controlled substances.[286] His brief was part of the 1,100 pages of briefs submitted to the court by both sides.

Eighmey charged that the government's case rehashed the arguments made at the district court level. He predicted that if the government outlawed the use of controlled substances to hasten death, physicians would administer these drugs illegally and surreptitiously.[287] Dr. Allison B. Willeford, a retired physician suffering from cancer, declared, "John Ashcroft should keep his hands off my personal choice."[288] Attorneys representing both sides prepared their cases.

A three-judge panel from the Court of Appeals heard the government's appeal at the federal courthouse in Portland, Oregon, on 7 May 2003. The panel included Judges Richard Tallman, appointed by President Bill Clinton (D); Donald P. Lay, appointed by President Lyndon Johnson (D); and Clifford Wallace, appointed by President Richard Nixon (R). The judges questioned attorneys from both sides during the one-hour hearing.

Judge Tallman asked Katsas whether Ashcroft's decision would influence the use of drugs for pain management and if the US government had the right to regulate medical practice in Oregon. Wallace challenged Stutsman as to why physicians didn't use a substance not covered by the CSA, such as insulin, to help patients die. Stutsman replied that only controlled substances guaranteed a safe and humane death.[289]

Judge Lay asked if the plaintiffs had standing and if the plaintiffs filed the case in the proper court. Questions such as these, as well as the lack of understanding of Oregon's law evidenced by Wallace, worried Coombs Lee. She feared the decision would support Ashcroft. She considered an appeal to all eleven members of the Appellate Court or to the Supreme Court.

The Ninth Circuit Court did not announce its decision for over a year. Eighmey reported on 22 May 2004 that he had no inkling of when the Ninth Circuit Court would issue its decision.[290] The Court announced its decision four days later. A panel of three judges ruled that Ashcroft exceeded his authority, usurped the power of state legislatures, and interfered with democratic debate when he issued a memorandum in 2001 declaring that the Oregon Death with Dignity Act was not a legitimate medical practice.

Tallman noted in the majority opinion that Ashcroft lacked clear congressional authority and violated the language of the CSA."[291] He commented, "We take no position on the merits or morality of physician-assisted suicide. This case is simply about who gets to decide."[292] Wallace asserted in his minority opinion that Ashcroft's memorandum was legal because physicians could hasten death with substances such as insulin.[293]

Opponents expressed dismay. Hamilton described the decision as "amazing and flawed."[294] Langlois of the *Catholic Sentinel* predicted that Ashcroft would appeal the decision to the Supreme Court, where Justice Kennedy, a Catholic, might provide the vote needed to overturn the decision.[295]

Proponents like Coombs Lee announced, "We won!"[296] A spokesperson for Oregon's Attorney General described the ruling as a "slam-dunk victory"[297] Stutsman, one of the attorneys for the plaintiffs, stated, "It's one victory in a long chain of victories. We've won two elections. We've won many legal battles at the state and federal level. This is just one more, perhaps it will be the last."[298]

Stutsman's statement proved wishful thinking. The three judges who issued the ruling denied Ashcroft's petition for a rehearing before all eleven members of the Ninth Circuit Court of Appeals. At that point, Ashcroft petitioned the US Supreme Court. On 26 February 2005, the highest court in the land agreed to hear the case, scheduling oral arguments for 5 October 2005.

Conclusion

Plaintiffs like Holmes and Romney fought Ashcroft's interpretation of the CSA, procured legal prescriptions, and died without using them. Judges of the District Court and Appellate Court agreed that Ashcroft overstepped his authority, especially as Congress declined to legislate the matter. The Oregon Death with Dignity Act remained in force after favorable decisions in District Court and the Ninth Circuit Court of Appeals. Attorney General Ashcroft appealed the case to the Supreme Court.[299]

The Oregon Department of Human Services collected evidence that people in other states and nations could view. Four years of statistics showed that the law worked well, and few people used it. Researchers like Dr. Linda Ganzini of the Oregon Health & Science University conducted scientific surveys. One of her studies, published in the *Journal of the American Medical Association*, indicated that Oregon's law improved patient healthcare.[300] Foes of the Oregon Death with Dignity Act contested the meaning of these statistics in light of the documented "abuses of assisted suicide in Oregon."[301]

The debate and experimentation envisioned by the Supreme Court continued. Radio talk show hosts and newspaper reporters interviewed people like Holmes and Romney. Popular magazines like *Readers Digest, People Magazine, AARP Magazine,* and *Oprah Magazine* educated the public about the choices people make before they die. Americans focused their attention to the coming battle in the Supreme Court.

Chapter 7

"It's a Hard Case": *Gonzales v. Oregon* (2006)

Introduction

The Supreme Court agreed to hear Attorney General Ashcroft's appeal of a District Court's decision that declared his memorandum illegal. They renamed the case *Gonzales v. Oregon* after Alberto Gonzales replaced Ashcroft as US Attorney General. This chapter discusses the passionate briefs, heated arguments, and controversial decision of the court. The nation's highest court does not operate in a vacuum. An incident occurred before they heard the case that focused the eyes of the nation on life-and-death issues.

Terri Schiavo

Terri Schiavo, a twenty-six-year-old Florida woman, experienced respiratory and cardiac arrest in 1990. Physicians diagnosed her as being in a persistent vegetative state. Her husband petitioned the courts to remove her feeding tube in 1998. Schiavo's parents disagreed, setting off a long legal battle. Social conservatives in Congress sponsored a bill that transferred jurisdiction of the case to the federal courts.

The bill passed the Senate on 20 March 2005. President Bush signed it the next day. However, the federal courts denied the petitions of Schiavo's parents, and the Supreme Court declined to hear the case. This allowed a Florida State court order to go into effect that allowed the removal of Schiavo's feeding tube. She died days later on 31 March 2005.[302] Polls indicated that most Americans agreed that Congress and President Bush acted too quickly and involved themselves in a personal matter. George Eighmey of Oregon Compassion & Choices observed, "I don't want politicians deciding my fate."[303]

The Schiavo case centered on the question of who makes a person's life-and-death decisions when he or she lacks the ability to do so. Oregon's law applies only to competent adults. Even so, Oregon's law invariably came up in discussions of the Schiavo case.[304] Don Colburn, a reporter for the *Oregonian*, noted that Oregonians discussed death and dying issues as early as 1991 in "legislative chambers, on the political stump, and around kitchen tables."[305] He argued that what happened in Florida would never happen in Oregon.

Gonzales v. Oregon (2006)

The appointment of a new chief justice added an element of unpredictability to the situation. Bush nominated John Roberts to the position after William Rehnquist's death in September 2005. During an interview, Senator Wyden asked Roberts about Oregon's law. Roberts stated that he believed a Supreme Court Judge should "start with the supposition that one has the right to be left alone."[306] Wyden voted for Roberts and the Senate confirmed him. Supporters of Oregon's law interpreted Roberts's statement to mean that he favored Oregon's law. When he voted otherwise, they charged that he deliberately mislead Wyden.[307]

Gonzales v. Oregon became the first major case heard under Roberts's leadership. Justice Anthony Kennedy observed, "For me, the case turns on the statute. It's a hard case."[308] The judges' heartfelt opinions on death and dying often crept into their arguments, even though they eventually decided on narrow legal grounds.[309]

Paul D. Clement, US Solicitor General, represented the petitioners. He asked the Supreme Court to rule on whether the US Attorney General permissibly construed the Controlled Substances Act (CSA) to prohibit the distribution of federally controlled substances for the purpose of facilitating an individual's suicide, regardless of a state law that authorized such distribution.[310] His succinct brief argued that the CSA established a comprehensive and uniform national system for regulating controlled substances. He maintained that tradition and authority supported Ashcroft's right to regulate the drugs used to hasten death in Oregon.[311]

The respondents consisted of the State of Oregon, represented by State Attorney General Hardy Myers; a group of physicians, pharmacists, and patients represented by Eli Stutsman; and seventeen patient-respondents, represented by Kathryn Tucker and Nicholas van Aelstyn of Compassion & Dying.

The brief of the State of Oregon contended that Ashcroft's threatened action would nullify the Oregon Death with Dignity Act and that neither the CSA nor its judicial interpretations suggested that Congress intended to displace the states' traditional power to regulate medical practice.[312]

Stutsman's brief noted that those he represented suffered likelihood of harm and therefore had standing. He argued that the Supreme Court ought to uphold the decisions of lower courts because Ashcroft's directive violated the language of the CSA, overstepped the bounds of the Attorney General's statutory authority, and contravened the intent of Congress.[313]

Nicholas van Aelstyn and Tucker, counsels for Compassion in Dying, submitted a brief on behalf of seventeen individuals. They did not use the terms "suicide" or "assisted suicide" in reference to Oregon's law. Instead, they referred to qualified Oregonians empowered by the law to choose the time, place, and manner of their impending deaths.[314] In addition, they contended that Ashcroft ignored a wealth of information in the annual reports of the Oregon Department of Human Services (DHS) that showed that the Act worked well.[315]

Tucker filed a motion to allow lawyers from each of the three respondents to present oral arguments before the Court and additional time to prepare their arguments. The Supreme Court denied her motion. This meant that Robert N. Atkinson, Deputy Attorney General for the State of Oregon, spoke for all the respondents during his allotted thirty-minute period.

Friends of the Court Briefs

A group of representatives to Congress stated in their brief that they gave Ashcroft the power to play an active role in regulating controlled substances.[316] The Catholic Medical Association Brief argued that, if the State of Oregon prevailed, it would undermine the authority of the federal government and make drug enforcement impossible.[317]

Physicians for Compassionate Care charged that the annual reports issued by the Oregon Department of Human Services (DHS) omitted information that proved Oregon's law was not legitimate medical practice. They cited as an example a case that cast doubt about the safeguards in the Oregon Death with Dignity Act. Hamilton claimed that Dave Freeland, a sixty-three-year-old man with lung cancer, received a lethal prescription, when what he needed was proper medical care and treatment for depression.[318]

The Strange Case of Dave Freeland

Freeland tried to call a right-to-die group, Compassion in Dying, on 20 April 2000, but mistakenly dialed a right-to-life group with a similar name, Physicians for Compassionate Care. Hamilton's wife, Cathy, took the call, counseled Freeland, and promised to keep in touch. Freeland eventually contacted Compassion in Dying. In 2001, Dr. Peter Reagan determined that he met the law's guidelines, secured a second opinion, and wrote a legal lethal prescription. A year and a half later, the Hamiltons visited Freeland and found him alone, dehydrated, and afraid to take his pain medication. They secured hospice care for Freeland and provided him with a convenient means of delivery for his pain medication. Freeland died of lung cancer in 2003.[319]

The Oregon DHS has a record of Freeland's request for a lethal prescription, his physician writing it, and a pharmacist filling it. However, as the DHS collects statistics only on those who die using Oregon's law, they have no record of the circumstances of his death.[320] Freeland's story, as described in the brief to the US Supreme Court, rests on the Hamiltons' version of events. Eighmey of Compassion in Dying stated that he could not refute their charges because of confidentiality laws.[321]

A number of friends of the court briefs presented additional arguments. The brief of the American Civil Liberties Union noted that the evidence in the annual Oregon DHS report "belied the doomsday prophecies" made by opponents of Oregon's law.[322] The American Public Health Association argued that vanguard states produce innovations in health care. The brief of Autonomy, Inc. quoted from Justice John Paul Stevens's decision in *Glucksberg* that "those who consider hastening their deaths do not face a choice of whether to live, only of how to die."[323]

The authors of friends of the court briefs wrote with skill and passion. They detailed a wide range of arguments that tell much about the concerns of interest groups. Petitioners and respondents employed moving stories and referred to the annual report of the Oregon DHS. The court showed that it valued input from interest groups by extending the time period during which they could submit briefs on two different occasions. The remarks and written opinions of the Supreme Court judges indicated that they listened to these arguments.[324]

Arguments Before the Supreme Court

The Supreme Court of the United States heard oral arguments in the case of *Gonzales v. Oregon* on 5 October 1995. Paul Clement, US Solicitor General, spoke for the plaintiffs. He contended that it would create a precedent for other states if the Court permitted Oregon to deviate from the standards established by the CSA. Justice Ruth Bader Ginsburg interrupted him to note that the decision in *Washington v. Glucksberg* stated that "physician-assisted suicide was a matter for the states."[325]

Judge Stevens declared that Congress passed the CSA to fight drug abuse, not to regulate the practice of medicine in the states. Judge David Souter questioned whether physicians could use drugs other than controlled substances to hasten death. Clement observed that Kevorkian, the "notorious proponent of assisted suicide," hadn't used them.[326] Ginsburg asked Clement to explain his remark. He replied that no factual records existed on whether physicians could use substances not controlled by the CSA for aid in dying under Oregon's law.

The judges initially couldn't hear Atkinson, the attorney for the State of Oregon. Justice Antonin Scalia elicited laughter when he observed, "You're too tall" (for the microphone).[327] Atkinson adjusted the microphone and delivered one sentence before Roberts asked, "If one state can say it's legal for doctors to prescribe morphine to make people feel better, or to prescribe steroids for bodybuilding, doesn't that undermine the uniformity of the federal law and make enforcement impossible?"[328]

Atkinson argued that it depended on how that state defined legitimate medical practice. At that point, Judges Sandra Day O'Connor and Scalia peppered Atkinson with questions. Judge Stephen Breyer asked, "Suppose I disagreed with you about that, would you lose the case?" Atkinson replied, "I would certainly lose ground, Your Honor."[329] Things went better toward the end of Atkinson's argument. He agreed with Stevens and Souter that Congress had not spoken on the issue of using controlled substances to legally hasten death.[330]

Clements struck back aggressively during the time that he reserved for rebuttal. He charged that the respondents "embraced the logical consequences of their position," one that denied the government the power to regulate controlled substances.[331]

Atkinson noted that that the judges' questions were not a reliable indicator of their final opinion. "They will push someone very hard and then write an opinion supporting their position."[332] Tucker observed that Atkinson might have made a better case had he discussed the human impact of the judges' decision.

The Court Decides

The Court would have reheard the case if the decision rested solely on the vote of retiring Judge Sandra Day O'Connor. However, on 17 January 2006, the Court announced a six to three decision in favor of the State of Oregon.

Justice Kennedy wrote the majority opinion, joined by Justices Stevens, O'Connor, Souter, Ginsberg, and Breyer. "The Controlled Substances Act does not allow the Attorney General to prohibit doctors from prescribing drugs for use in physician-assisted suicide under state laws permitting the procedure."[333] Kennedy excoriated Ashcroft for acting without authority in an area in which he was not competent. He upbraided him for faulty decision making, breaking his promise to consult with local authorities, and disrespecting the State of Oregon.[334]

The court did not accept the validity of the argument made by the Ninth Circuit Court and Atkinson. It rejected their claim that Ashcroft's memorandum unconstitutionally encroached on the domain of the state—the practice of medicine. The court concluded that there was no question that the federal government can set standards in these areas.

Justice Scalia, a conservative Catholic, termed suicide immoral in his dissenting opinion.[335] He insisted that the definitions of the words "prescriptions" and "medical" meant that physicians could prescribe only substances that treated a disease.[336] The substances used by physicians under Oregon's law did not treat disease and therefore were illegal. He cited the brief of the Pro-Life Legal Defense Fund as authority for this argument.[337]

Judge Clarence Thomas pointed out the Court's inconsistency of ruling in *Raich v. Gonzales* (2005) that the CSA overrode California's medical marijuana law, but in *Gonzales v. Oregon* the CSA did not override Oregon's Death with Dignity Act.[338] Thomas dissented from the Court's decision in *Raich*. He argued that the Court should limit the power of the CSA in a manner consistent with federalism. He wrote his own dissent in *Oregon v. Gonzales*. He offered the curious argument that the Supreme Court should follow the precedent established in *Raich*, even though he believed the Court erred in that decision.[339]

Proponents of Oregon's law were ecstatic at the Court's decision. Charlene Andrews, a breast cancer patient and plaintiff in the case, offered a toast in a moment of triumph. "I am just elated this part is over, and I feel the US Supreme Court did justice in recognizing the feelings and needs of people who have terminal illness, to be able to use that process in a compassionate and dignified manner." [340] Governor Ted Kulangoski (D) declared the decision a victory for the voters of Oregon that recognized the right of the states to act as "crucibles of change."[341]

President Bush expressed disappointment with the ruling and reaffirmed his commitment to building a culture of life. Diane Coleman of Not Dead Yet grumbled, "Both the Department of Justice and the Supreme Court have failed us."[342] Doerflinger, of the US Conference of Catholic Bishops, argued that the decision merely changed the forum from the courts back to Congress.[343]

The most important effect of the court's decision was that Oregonians who chose to hasten their death could continue to do so. A ruling for the petitioners would have placed their lives and deaths in a limbo of legal confusion. Matthew Staver, president of the Liberty Counsel, observed, "This particular case was either going to close the door or open it, and it opened it."[344]

Senator Hatch predicted that Congress would solve the problems created by the court's decision.[345] In October 2006 Senator Sam Brownback (R-KS), a presidential aspirant, introduced legislation that prohibited physicians from prescribing federally controlled substances for the purpose of hastening death. The editors of the *Mail Tribune* advised him to "butt out."[346] Wyden placed the bill on legislative hold.[347] Brownback acknowledged his bill had little chance of passing and looked forward to a debate with Wyden sometime in the future.[348]

Conclusion

The Supreme Court decision ended the legal debate over Oregon's Death with Dignity Act at a time when the Schiavo case focused the country's feelings on death and dying issues. Changes in the composition of the Supreme Court increased the uncertainty of the outcome of *Gonzales v. Oregon*. The briefs and amicus curiae written to the judges outlined the basic issues in the cultural war over death.

The oral arguments helped judges appraise the positions of their fellow judges and informed them on policy ramifications of their decision not discussed in briefs. However, the judges and their clerks do much of the work of the court behind the scenes. They undoubtedly discussed the difficulties of deciding a moral issue. In the end, the judges based their decision on whether a federal official exceeded his authority.

Several groups viewed the court's decision as a victory. Terminal patients expressed satisfaction that they could control the time and means of their deaths. Right-to-die advocates showed renewed interest in sponsoring similar legislation in other states. Eighmey observed, "At this point the momentum is going to change."[349] Oregonians felt that the court vindicated the decisions the voters had made in two elections. Kennedy's stern rebuke of the attorney general for exceeding his powers pleased advocates of individual and states' rights.

The court made its decision in *Gonzales v. Oregon* on very narrow grounds. Federal executive agencies that used due deliberation could regulate practice in Oregon through administrative rules. Opponents might still convince Congress to amend the CSA to establish standards for the use of controlled substances that supersede state regulations. Right-to-life advocates rededicated themselves to ending Oregon's experiment by passing legislation in Congress similar to Brownback's bill.

Marcia Angell of the Harvard Medical School predicted, "It is likely that physician-assisted suicide will gradually become widely available, state by state."[350] States receptive to innovation renewed their interest in Death with Dignity bills and initiatives. Opponents of hastened death legislation marshaled their forces to foil these attempts. They had suffered defeats in the past in Oregon, in Congress, and in the courts, but they were successful in blocking bills and initiatives in other states. They did not intend for this to change.

Part III. Involving Other States:

Successive Adoption

Chapter 8–10

Legislation in Other States: Oregonians Blaze a Trail

Introduction

Faye Girsh, executive director of the Hemlock Society USA, noted that Oregon's law was "a model for the rest of the country, if not the world." [351] On the other hand, right-to-life advocates warned that the "mind-set of evil" was "alive and well."[352] Right-to-die supporters sponsored initiatives in Michigan (1998) and Maine (2000), as well as bills in the legislatures of Hawaii (2002), California (2006), and Vermont (2006). This chapter tells the story of their attempts to implement Death with Dignity in these states.

Michigan

Ed Pierce, a retired physician, founded a group called Merian's Friends. He named the group after a woman that Dr. Kevorkian helped to die. Pierce asked Stutsman of the National Death with Dignity Center for help in passing legislation. Stutsman expressed reservations about the chances of passing an initiative in Michigan but promised financial help.[353] Merian's Friends collected signatures for a prescription-only initiative called Proposal B. They collected $1,077,494.15, but spent $200,000 getting the measure on the ballot.[354] This meant they had less funds to answer their opponents' charges.[355]

Those opposed to Proposal B formed the Coalition for Compassionate Care. It included the Catholic, Baptist, and Lutheran Churches, the Michigan Medical Society, and the Governor's Committee on Disability. They collected $5,375,442.76.[356] One of their ads showed the scales of Justice with the Coalition members on one side and Proposal B on the other. Another depicted the Hippocratic Oath in flames.[357]

Michigan voters defeated Proposal B by a 71-29 percent margin on 2 November 1998. Voters cast 2,116,154 "No" votes and 859,381 "Yes" votes.[358] Solid majorities in all age groups opposed the measure.[359] Several reasons account for this result. The proposal title mentioned suicide, an inflammatory choice of words. Kevorkian's activities tarnished the supporters' reputation. The Catholic Church mobilized parishioners in a state where 23 percent of the people identified as Catholic.[360] Finally, advocates failed to obtain the backing of key state officials and the medical community.[361] Stutsman observed that Michigan showed that an underfunded, well-intentioned campaign was no match for a well-funded and organized campaign.[362] Death with Dignity supporters fared better in Maine.

Maine

Mainers for Death with Dignity (Yes On 1), a coalition of right-to-die groups, sponsored an initiative petition for the Maine Death with Dignity Act in 2000. They expressed optimism, even though 44 percent of Mainers were Catholic.[363] Maine was a progressive state, open to innovation. Polls showed that 70 percent of those surveyed favored such legislation. Mainers for Death with Dignity collected $1,631,497.71 for the campaign.[364]

Opponents formed the No On 1 coalition. Members included the Maine Medical Association, Home Hospice Care, Right to Life, and the Catholic Diocese. Early polls showed this group's cause fifty points behind.[365] No On 1 raised, $957,474.[366] Two other political action committees raised funds to defeat the Maine Death with Dignity Act. The Coalition for Compassionate Care for the Dying reported contributions of $1,049,692.72, and the Respect Life Educational Foundation indicated receipts of $1,113,958.38.[367]

Bishop Joseph Gerry, of the Diocese of Portland, sent a video to each parish that urged parishioners to vote against the proposal. No On 1 sponsored a number of commercials. One attacked the "euphemisms" used in the proposal. One ad showed gowned and masked medical professionals wheeling a patient into an emergency room. Dr. Thomas Reardon, an Oregon physician, provided this narration. "After taking this medication some patients in Oregon had complications so disturbing that family members called 911."[368]

Yes On 1 asked television stations not to air ads that presented false information. The stations pulled one ad until No On 1 provided documentation.

Yes On 1 countered with ads that featured Kitzhaber, Governor of Oregon, and Coombs Lee, of Compassion & Choices. They refuted the charges made by the No On 1 coalition, but it was too late.

The measure failed by a margin of 51-49 percent. The vote was 315,031 in favor and 332,280 against.[369] The No On 1 Coalition shared the credit for their come-from-behind victory with its member groups. Advertising provided the margin of victory. The following year both sides united to pass two bills in the state legislature that funded hospice care and provided funds for education and research to improve end-of-life care. Death with Dignity advocates came even closer to victory in Hawaii.

Hawaii

The first right-to-die legislation in Hawaii was a 1976 bill that reinforced the principle that physicians need not take extraordinary measures to prolong life. The bill foundered in committee. Governor Benjamin J. Cayetano (D), the first governor of Filipino descent, convened an eighteen-member Blue Ribbon committee to consider death and dying issues in 1996.

The committee recommended better hospice care, mandated pain management, and improved advance directives. They upheld the ban on euthanasia. They believed that a bill that authorized lethal injection did not stand a chance of passing the legislature, and that patient-administered lethal prescriptions had a chance of passing. At the committee's urging, the legislature strengthened living wills, required the Department of Motor Vehicles to ask applicants if they had an advance healthcare directive, and funded hospice care.[370]

Six assisted suicide bills failed to get out of committee between 1998 and 2002. Much of the credit for their defeat goes to Hawaii's Partnership for Appropriate and Compassionate Care, a coalition of eleven medical, hospice, and religious groups. Kelly M. Rosati, Executive Director of Hawaii Family Forum, served as coalition spokesperson. Deacon Walter Yoshimitsu, manager of diocesan services for the Catholic Diocese of Hawaii, provided political expertise.[371]

The Compassion in Dying Federation established an affiliate in Hawaii in 2002 that linked their legal advocacy in rainy Oregon to lobbying in tropical Hawaii. They formed a coalition of eleven organizations called Hawaii Death with Dignity. Scott Foster, a public relations expert, served as communications director. Roland L. Halpern, Executive Director of Hawaii Compassion in Dying, provided leadership. Andi van der Voort, President of the Hemlock Society, furnished funds and assistance.

Eric Hamakawa (D-South Hilo-Puna) introduced the "Hawaii Death with Dignity Act" into the House in February 2002. The House Judiciary committee passed the bill after a three-hour hearing and sent it to the floor where it passed 30 to 20.[372]

David Matsuura (D-South Hilo-Puna), chairman of the Senate Health Committee, expressed his opinion of the bill when it reached his desk. "Absolutely, I will not hear assisted suicide. This dumb bill wasn't even on our radar screen. I haven't even looked at the measure or studied this measure yet. I can't figure out what assisted suicide is."[373] Cayetano hoped that Matsuura would rise above his personal beliefs and schedule a hearing.

Matsuura gutted the bill and inserted language that addressed shortcomings in the state's advance directives law. During testimony, he pointed to two large stacks of correspondence on his desk and observed that the stack against Death with Dignity looked higher than the one for it. Halpern reviewed the materials in both stacks. The large stack contained duplicate letters and books that padded the stack and distorted the comparison.[374]

Cayetano asked Matsuura to discharge the original Hawaii Death with Dignity bill after hearing that a federal court issued an injunction barring enforcement of Attorney General Ashcroft's ruling against Oregon's law. Matsuura sent the bill to the Senate on 30 April 2002. They approved it on the second of three required readings by a 13-12 vote, and set the final vote for Thursday, 2 May 2002.[375]

Rosati warned her supporters that Hawaii was close to becoming the second state to approve assisted suicide legislation. Representatives of the Catholic Church hand-carried letters from Bishop Francis X. DiLorenzo, urging senators to vote no on the bill. Proponents canvassed neighborhoods and inundated legislators with personal visits, phone calls, and e-mails. When asked about the bill's prospects, Foster observed, "It's anyone's guess. It really is."[376]

Cayetano stood by to sign the bill into law if it passed the Senate. After two hours of heart-rending debate, the Senate rejected it by a 14–11 vote on the afternoon of the final day of the 2002 session. Three members, who had previously voted for the measure, changed their votes. Cayetano appeared crestfallen but praised the high level of debate.[377]

The Democratic platform in 2003 supported adoption by the legislature of the Hawaii Death with Dignity Act.[378] The Republican platform did not mention the issue. However, their gubernatorial candidate, Linda Lingle, strongly opposed hastened death. David Shapiro of the *Honolulu Advertiser* argued that Lingle's position was at odds with her belief that individuals should enjoy freedom from government control.[379]

State Senator Colleen Hanabusa (D-Nanakuli-Waianae-Makaha) introduced a Death with Dignity Act bill in 2003. Opponent's launched a $40,000 ad campaign.[380] DiLorenzo sent a letter to legislators that stated his opposition, along with Foley and Hendin's book entitled *The Case Against Assisted Suicide: For the Right to End-of-Life Care.* The bill died in committee.

State Representatives voted a Death with Dignity bill out of committee in 2004 but returned it to committee after a discussion on the floor of the House.[381] They cited Lingle's opposition and election year fears as reasons for their inaction. Halpern urged right-to-die advocates to wait until the following year.[382]

The legislators of Hawaii talked story, a form of communication that involves sharing personal experiences as a way of building relationships. When one listens respectfully and nonjudgmentally, it fosters collaboration.[383] Frank and open discussions brought a renewed emphasis on palliative care. Lobbyists united to persuade the legislature to fund hospices, and to support living wills, powers of attorney, and counseling for the dying.[384] Kathryn Tucker, Director of Legal Affairs for Compassion & Choices, argued before a panel of lawyers and physicians in 2011 that nothing in standard medical practice prohibited Hawaiian physicians from providing patients with prescriptions that hastened their deaths.[385] A far different picture emerged in the large, complex state of California.

California

Supporters of hastened death legislation in California advanced their interests through an initiative petition, bills in the legislative assembly, and legal action. The Americans Against Human Suffering qualified an initiative that allowed lethal injections for terminal patients in 1992. After its defeat, Death with Dignity supporters sponsored bills patterned after Oregon's law in almost every session of the state legislature.

The Terri Schiavo Case and the *Gonzales* decision in 2005 reenergized right-to-die advocates. A Field poll showed seven out of ten Californians supported providing the terminally ill with a legal way to hasten death.[386] Assemblyperson Patty Berg (D-Eureka) commented, "We're working closely with Oregon, and we've had a couple other states interested in working with us as well, because as California goes, so goes the rest of the nation."[387]

Berg and Lloyd Levine (D-San Fernando) sponsored the California Compassionate Choice Act (AB651) in 2006. One hundred twenty people attended the hearing, but the bill failed to gain approval in the Senate Judiciary committee. Berg noted, "Public opinion is with us. We'll come a little closer to victory the next time this bill comes up."[388]

Berg and Levine introduced a similar bill, AB 374, in 2007. It also failed to get out of committee. Levine commented, "We really had two main groups working against us: the Catholic Church and disability-rights folks."[389] These activists asserted that their credibility lay in their ability to reach liberals and moderates with the message that if such a bill passed, health maintenance organizations would force the disabled to end their lives to save money.

Kathryn Tucker of Compassion & Choices litigated on behalf of patients and a physician in California. She filed suit over the pain treatment of Lester Tomlinson in 2003.[390] As a result, the Medical Board reprimanded Tomlinson's physician, Dr. Eugene Whitney, for undertreatment of pain and recommended revocation of his license to practice medicine.[391]

Tucker defended Dr. Harold Luke before the Medical Board in 2005. The case involved charges by a nurse that he prescribed too much morphine. Tucker argued that every physician who treated a dying patient was at risk if the board second-guessed their intent.[392] The Board reversed its decision to revoke Luke's license. Advocates of Death with Dignity applauded these decisions and looked eastward to a state with a reputation for independence.

Vermont

Dick Walters, a retired merchandise manager, met with several people in his living room. He and his friends agreed that a dedicated group could convince the legislature to pass legislation modeled on Oregon's law.[393] Vermont was a progressive state. Although 38 percent of Vermonters were Catholic, 22 percent of the population identified with no religion.[394] They incorporated Vermont Death with Dignity in October 2002 and sponsored bills in the Legislative Assembly from 2003 to 2006.[395]

The Legislative Council of Vermont issued a report, "Oregon's Death with Dignity Law and Euthanasia in the Netherlands: Factual Disputes" (2004), at the request of a number of legislators. Their report concluded that many of the issues in the Netherlands depended on how one interpreted the evidence and that it was apparent that Oregon's Act enhanced the options of the dying in that state.[396]

Representative Ann Pugh (D-South Burlington) introduced the Vermont Death with Dignity Bill (H168) in 2005. The bill died on a tie vote in the Human Affairs Committee.[397] Dr. Robert Orr of the Vermont Alliance for Ethical Healthcare and Bishop Kenneth A. Angell of the Diocese of Burlington led the campaign against the bill. Angell insisted, "The Oregon Death with Dignity Act attempts to exonerate and absolve the patient from the sin of suicide."[398]

Representative William Aswad (D-Burlington) introduced the Patient Choice and Control at End of Life Act (H 44) on 12 January 2007.[399] Vermont Death with Dignity solicited funds and hired a professional team of lobbyists. They commissioned a professional advertising campaign that featured endorsements by former Vermont Governors Phil Hoff and Madeleine Kunin. They paid for a Zogby International poll, which showed that 82 percent of those surveyed favored legislation that allowed patients to hasten their deaths with a legal lethal prescription.

Several Representatives observed that the bill would pass the legislature, but Governor Jim Douglas (R) would veto it.[400] There were ninety-three Democrats, forty-nine Republicans, six progressives, and two independents in the House. It took fifty-one votes to sustain the veto. Pro-lifers were afraid that they could not count on that number.[401]

Over 350 spectators jammed the ornate House of Representatives to hear testimony before the House Judiciary Committee on 21 March 2007. Supporters of the bill wore green stickers that read, "Listen to the Patient." Opponents wore yellow stickers that proclaimed, "I Oppose Physician-Assisted Suicide." Barbara Roberts, former governor of Oregon, argued in favor of the bill. Orr countered, "If a patient wants to hasten death, he or she merely needs to stop eating and drinking."[402]

The House of Representatives voted against the bill by an 82-63 margin after four hours of debate. Only three Republicans voted for the bill, and Democrats were divided. Rep. Harvey Otterman (R-Topsham) believed that "the bill went too far in enforcing one group's preferences on the traditional values of others."[403] Walters believed that the vast majority of Vermonters wanted Death with Dignity legislation and promised that his group would continue its efforts.[404]

Opponents of the bill mobilized their supporters. They generated an unprecedented number of calls, e-mails, and letters against the bill. Legislators noted that those who contacted them often referred to information contained in a pamphlet published in Oregon entitled "Oregon's Assisted Suicide Experience: Safeguards Don't Work."[405]

Walters promised his group would do better the next time. He formed a coalition of right-to-die groups called Patient Choices at the End of Life. The board of directors of this new group considered a stronger stand against the message of the Catholic Church and a coordinated effort to motivate supporters to contact their legislators in the next campaign. However, Michael Sorokin, whose firm managed the lobbying campaign in the legislature, observed that Death with Dignity legislation stood a much better chance of success in the state of Washington.[406]

Conclusion

Charles Bentz, president of Physicians for Compassionate Care (PCC), urged supporters to "Avoid euphemisms. Call it what it is: physician-assisted suicide."[407] William Toffler, national director of PCC, advised them to develop coalitions with religious, right-to-life, and disability groups and to use the power of the Catholic Church to raise money and exert influence. Bishops in Hawaii, Maine and Vermont made effective personal appeals to parishioners and legislators. In addition, Toffler's group developed their own interpretation of data collected by the Oregon Department of Human Affairs to convince voters and legislators to vote against Death with Dignity.[408]

Eli Stutsman, president of the board of the National Death with Dignity Center, detailed the strategy used by proponents of Death with Dignity.

He stressed coalition building and gaining the support of civic leaders and groups.[409] He believed in the effectiveness of legal challenges directed toward opponent's financial irregularities and misrepresentations. He proclaimed the value of press releases and cultivating the media.[410] He realized attacks on the Church would promote a backlash, but his supporters did not always follow his advice.

The Oregon experience applied more to initiative campaigns than legislative contests. Both sides tailored their tactics to win over individual legislators in Hawaii, California, and Vermont. Proponents found governors excellent spokespersons. They found it difficult to sway legislators confronted by a disciplined and committed minority that had the power to ensure that those who opposed them were not reelected.

Stutsman noted, "Reform efforts elsewhere cannot simply copy the Oregon law and expect to succeed."[411] Each state has different population characteristics and propensity to adopt innovative legislation.[412] Jack Walker, a political scientist at the University of Michigan, confirms Stutsman's assertion that it makes sense to focus on innovative states that have a high percentage of people who do not identify with any religion.[413]

Events in all five states show that oppositional interest groups can work together to improve conditions for the dying. In Vermont, both sides cooperated in writing S. 281, an act that created a legislative study committee on palliative care and management of chronic pain.[414] It required state agencies and stakeholders to collaborate on a written report.[415]

Twenty-two states have considered Death with Dignity initiatives or bills. These campaigns showed many similarities. Polls initially indicated that the issue enjoyed strong support. However, opponents used key political and medical groups, advertising, and the power of the pulpit to chip away at that support. The next chapter tells how two states adopted similar legislation eleven years after Oregon's law went into effect.

Chapter 9

Victory on Two Fronts: Washington and Montana

Introduction

Oregon voters passed the Death with Dignity Act in 1994, and it went into effect in 1997 after a favorable court decision in *Washington v. Glucksberg.* It took eleven years before another state followed suit. In 2008, Washington voters adopted a right-to-die initiative, and a Montana judge ruled that individuals had the right to hasten their deaths under that state's constitution.

Deborah Stone, a political scientist and independent scholar, stated in *Policy Paradox* that policymaking "is a constant struggle over the criteria for classification, the boundaries of categories, and the definition of ideals that guide the way people behave."[416] Mark Moore of the Kennedy School of Government, in *Creating Public Value,* refers to the "rigidity and relentlessness" of right-to-life groups.[417] These groups formed coalitions, raised tremendous amounts of money, and were parties to every legal case. They defeated repeated attempts to pass right-to-die legislation.

Two interest groups led the fight for Death with Dignity legislation. Eli Stutsman of the National Death with Dignity Center expressed his admiration for Moore's use of analytical techniques.[418] Stutsman hired a nationally known polling company to determine the prospects of success for an initiative. They determined that Washingtonians were receptive to the concept of hastened death.

Kathryn Tucker, legal counsel for Compassion & Choices, knew Montana was ripe for a legal challenge. She unsuccessfully argued a similar case, *Sampson vs. the State of Alaska* (2001) before the Alaska Supreme Court. She worked with local attorneys on a *Montana Law Review* article. Stutsman and Tucker overcame the fervid opposition of right-to-life groups. As a result of their efforts, two more states adopted Death with Dignity legislation.

Washington (2008)

Stutsman learned from his experience working for a 1991 Washington initiative that people found the notion of lethal injections abhorrent. He made certain that the Oregon and Washington Death with Dignity Acts provided only for lethal prescriptions. Stutsman found a formidable spokesperson for his cause in popular former governor Booth Gardner (D). Gardner underwent brain surgery during the campaign. Afterward he observed, "When I go I want to decide."[419]

Yes on I-1000 Committee

Supporters of the Washington Death with Dignity Act formed the Yes on I-1000 Committee in February 2008. Anne Martens, the group's communication director, believed their chances of success were good because of similar demographics in Oregon and Washington. The two states ranked at the bottom of the list of people affiliated with a religion.[420] Revelations of priest abuse of children in both states tarnished the reputation of the Catholic Church. Lawsuits by the victims brought Northwest dioceses to insolvency or the brink of bankruptcy.

The Yes on I-1000 Committee hired two consulting firms to manage a signature gathering campaign that used volunteer and paid signature-gatherers. They collected 100,000 more signatures than the 225,000 necessary to qualify the initiative for the ballot. The Washington Secretary of State certified the initiative for the ballot on 13 August 2008.

Chris Carlson of Spokane, who has Parkinson's disease, chaired the No on Initiative 1000 Coalition. The group's website featured the names of members of the community, elected leaders, physicians, and members of the disability community opposed to I-1000. The coalition condemned proponents of the initiative for raising funds outside the state, especially those from the Death with Dignity National Center headed by Stutsman.

The Yes on Initiative 1000 Committee counterattacked. They pointed to contributions from Archdioceses in Denver, Cincinnati, and Venice (Florida) to the No on I-1000 campaign. Martens charged, "Clearly it's more important to them to impose their religious beliefs on the people of Washington than it is to take care of the victims of abuse in their own states."[421] Carlson labeled these remarks "thinly disguised anti-Catholic bigotry."[422]

The No on I-1000 Coalition

Dominican Sister Sharon Park of the Western Washington State Catholic Conference explained that state election law permitted churches to distribute educational but not advocacy materials. The No on I-1000 Coalition paid for two DVDs, brochures, and envelopes to collect funds sent to the 290 parishes of the Archdiocese of Seattle. The DVD "In God's Time" accurately explained the Church's moral and ethical teaching on end-of-life issues.[423]

Park observed that the priest or pastor might say something, during Catholic services.[424] Several speakers mentioned their intention was to inform parishioners' consciences and not to tell them how to vote. Sister Francine Barber reminded one congregation that "no one, not even the Church," could do that.[425] Deacon Bill Haines and his wife Gina Washington warned parishioners, "Don't be deceived into thinking this is just a 'choice' issue."[426] Father Scott Connolly argued that terms were important. "While they refer to it as 'death with dignity,' it's assisted suicide."[427]

The Coalition Against Assisted Suicide and the No on Assisted Suicide PAC raised $1,310,616.26. The Roman Catholic Church and its affiliates contributed nearly two-thirds of the total. The largest donation was a $275,000 from the New Haven, Connecticut, Knights of Columbus. The Seattle Diocese gave $50,000, and the Diocese of Portland, Oregon, gave $5,000.[428]

Alex Morgan, campaign manager for the Yes on I-1000 Committee, noted the ability of his opponents to raise money from archdioceses across the country. He commented, "We are far and away the underdogs in this campaign."[429] Despite his assertion, right-to-die supporters raised more money than their opponents. Compassion & Choices Washington and the Yes on I-1000 Committee raised $5,517,634.83. Gardner, heir to the Weyerhaeuser Timber fortune, and his family contributed $750,000. The Oregon Death with Dignity fund donated $615,000. Loren Parks, an Oregon businessman, gave $250,000. More than 60 percent of the funds came from outside Washington.

The Campaign

Fletcher, Rowley, Chao, and Riddle, Inc., an award winning consulting firm, coordinated media efforts for the Yes on I-1000 Committee. Their message appeared in a number of venues. The editors of the *Seattle Times* wrote, "Death with dignity is a right that should be allowed."[430] A concerned citizen wrote a letter to the *Seattle Times*. "My life does not belong to the state or the church. It does not belong to my neighbors, my parents, and my children or my spouse."[431] A webpage developed by Northwest Passage Counseling debunked fifty-four of the opposition's "lies."[432]

The Yes on I-1000 Committee aired two television spots and a radio ad in late October, aimed at undecided voters. Former governor of Oregon, Barbara Roberts (D), defended Oregon's law in "Getting the Facts Straight."[433] Another television ad featured a physician whose mother legally hastened her death in Oregon.[434] Despite their lead in a late October poll, proponents feared a last-minute media blitz by their opponents.

The No on I-1000 Coalition hired actor Martin Sheen, who portrayed the US president in the television series *West Wing*, to do a radio and television ad. He argued that I-1000 tells doctors it was acceptable to give a lethal drug overdose to a seriously ill person, even if he or she was depressed.[435]

Barbara Wagner, an Oregon cancer patient, asserted in another ad that a survey by Dr. Linda Ganzini proved that one-quarter of the patients who died under Oregon's law suffered from depression. (See chapter 10 for a discussion of this survey.) She claimed that she received letters from the Oregon Health Plan that stated they would pay for a lethal prescription, but not for drugs for her life-threatening illness.

Rheba De Tormay, professor emeritus of the University of Washington School of Nursing, told her story in another ad. She thanked God that her husband lived twenty-eight months after receiving a diagnosis from doctors of having three months to live.[436]

Proponents countered every assertion. The ad that dissected the Martin Sheen commercial showed a black screen after each of Sheen's statements and "Lie!" appeared in white. A voice-over provided the "facts." The narrator noted that, if there was any question of mental competence, the law required referral of the patient for a mental health evaluation. He declared independent studies showed that most patients who requested death with dignity were not depressed.[437]

Three former governors and the editors of ten of the state's leading newspapers endorsed the initiative. Washington's governor, Chris Gregoire (D), said that although she personally did not support the measure, she wouldn't actively work against it. Her spokesperson noted that Gregoire believed that this was a personal issue and "Voters in Washington will have to make up their own minds."[438] Opponents predicted, "It's going to be close."[439] Supporters thought they could see a win.[440]

The Vote

Washington voters approved the Death with Dignity law by a vote of 1,709,768 for and 1,247,121 against (58 to 42 percent) on 4 November 2008.[441] Martens observed that it was not the "normal east-west, urban-rural split" usually seen in Washington politics.[442] The initiative passed in thirty-one eastern and western counties. It failed in eight conservative central Washington counties in the rich agricultural region along the Columbia River.[443]

Voters in all but two of Washington's counties mailed in their ballots, so there were no exit polls. CNN News conducted a survey of 1,233 voters that showed that the profiles of Washington voters matched those of Oregonians, who voted on a similar measure in 1994 and 1997. More men favored I-1000 than women (60 percent to 54 percent). Supporters were liberal (80 percent) Democrats (74 percent), who did not identify with any religion (79 percent). Opponents identified themselves as conservative (67 percent), Republican (65 percent), and Catholic (53 percent) or born-again Evangelical (70 percent).[444]

The Yes on I-1000 Committee profited from the leadership monetary contributions of Stutsman and Gardner. The two signature-gathering firms got their message out early, and then mined the lists of signatures for donors. Their focused and responsive media campaign started early and stayed on the offense.

The efforts of the No on I-1000 Committee were underfunded and uncoordinated. Sister Sharon Parks delivered the Catholic vote, and the church hierarchy stayed in the background. The DVD "In God's Time" deserved play outside the Catholic community. Doctors Toffler, Stevens, and Bentz from Oregon each had an opinion letter published in the *Seattle Times*, but few local physicians were actively involved in the campaign.[445] Disability groups were quiet except for this statement from Not Dead Yet. "It's a mistake for the people of Washington to accept death as a progressive health care policy."[446]

The No on I-1000 Coalition used evidence from a survey by Dr. Linda Ganzini on the prevalence of depression among those who hastened their deaths. Proponents of the initiative countered this approach with the common sense assertion that yes, terminally ill patients often experience sadness and depression, but they are still capable of making informed decisions.

Carlson believed that money influenced the outcome of the campaign. He argued that the legislature was the proper place for legislation as complicated as the Washington Death with Dignity Act. He feared the passage of the initiative was a step toward euthanasia and urged those who opposed the initiative to advocate improved care for those at risk.[447] The State issued the statistics on the law ten months later. Thirty-six people hastened their death. They suffered from cancer (79%) and were from forty-eight to ninety-five years of age. Ninety percent were from western Washington.[448]

Leaders from both sides predicted that the approval of I-1000 by Washington voters had consequences for the rest of the nation. Rita Marker, of the International Euthanasia and Assisted Suicide Task Force, claimed that, "other states would fall like dominoes." A month later another state legalized hastened death.[449]

Montana (2008)

Kathryn Tucker, Compassion & Choices legal director, thought litigation in state courts could open the way for patients to access aid in dying. Tucker outlined her case in a 2007 *Montana Law Review* article.[450] She argued Montana courts would recognize an individual's choice to receive aid in dying because the state's constitution guaranteed rights of privacy and dignity well beyond those mentioned in the US Constitution. Montana's Constitution declares, "The dignity of the human being is inviolable," and the right of individual privacy "shall not be infringed without the showing of a compelling state interest."[451]

Robert Baxter swore in his affidavit dated 28 June 2008 to the Montana First Judicial Court that he was seventy-five years of age, a resident of Yellowstone County, and a retired long-haul trucker. He commented that his wife and four children supported him in the goals of the case. Baxter declared he was terminally ill with leukemia and asked the court for "the legal option of being able to die in a peaceful and dignified manner by consuming medication prescribed by my doctor for that purpose."[452]

Tucker and Mark S. Connell, a Montana attorney, argued the case on 10 October 2007. They represented Baxter, four Montana physicians, and Compassion & Choices. Jennifer M. Anders and Anthony Johnstone represented the state of Montana.

The plaintiffs challenged the constitutionality of homicide laws by the legislature as they applied to physician-assisted suicide. They requested a declaratory judgment that required the State of Montana to allow a "physician to provide aid in dying to a mentally competent, terminally ill adult patient facing a dying process the patient finds intolerable."[453] They asked that the defendants not charge physicians who provided such aid with a crime. Wesley J. Smith, a prominent right-to-life attorney, commented that "the case is certainly no sure thing—either way. But I do know it is likely to be a legal fight to the finish that could eventually grab the attention of the entire world."[454]

District Court Judge Dorothy McCarter noted in her decision on 5 December 2008 that the State Constitution reflected Montanans' "abhorrence and distrust of excessive government interference in their personal lives."[455] It differed from the constitutions of other states, because it used the term "inviolable" in its dignity clause.[456] She ruled that a competent terminally ill patient has the constitutional right to die with dignity and that physicians could prescribe such medication without fear of prosecution.[457] McCarter held the legislature responsible for implementing her decision.

Baxter never learned of his victory. He died in his sleep on the day McCarter announced her decision. Attorney General Mike McGrath requested a stay of decision in January 2009. He noted that the state had no safeguards or procedures in place to provide guidance and oversight for physicians. McCarter denied his request. Compassion & Choices sent a letter to Montana physicians. They reassured willing practitioners that it was safe to practice aid in dying and offered them established medical protocols.

McGrath appealed McCarter's decision to the Montana State Supreme Court. Right-to-die and right-to-life interest groups filed friends of the court briefs. Bishop George L. Thomas of Helena promised the Church's help in overturning the decision.[458] The Montana Supreme Court ruled on 31 December 2009 that nothing in the state constitution prevented patients from hastening their deaths and gave doctors the right to prescribe lethal medicine. Kathryn Tucker stated that she would have welcomed a broader ruling. The court did not guarantee a right to die and left the decision for such public policy to the people and legislature of Montana. In 2011, right-to-die advocates defeated two bills in the Montana State Senate that sought to reverse the court's decision.[459]

Conclusion

Eli Stutsman called the campaign in Washington "a wonderful accomplishment" but warned that political opposition remains high in many states.[460] Events in Washington and Montana increased the possibility, but not the probability, of other states passing such legislation. The Death with Dignity National Center is analyzing demographics, the cost of media advertising, and the results of polling in Arizona, Colorado, Maine, Massachusetts, Nevada, and Wyoming.[461] Hawaii and Vermont do not have the initiative process; however, they are also possibilities for success, if the Democratic Party controls their legislatures and captures their governorships.

Americans now have more options for dying. Hospice is commonplace. Palliative care is a board certified specialty. Physicians can legally pursue aggressive pain management, even if opiates or barbiturates hasten death. States can pass aid-in-dying laws. Patients may forgo or discontinue life-sustaining therapies. Voluntarily stopping eating and drinking is accepted as a natural part of the dying process. A panel of the American Medical Association endorsed sedation to the point of unconsciousness.[462] The dying in Oregon, Washington, and Montana now have one more option. They can obtain lethal prescriptions from their physician.

Chapter 10

Uncharted Waters: Ten Years of Reports and Scientific Surveys

Introduction

"What the hell happened? Why am I not dead?"[463] David Prueitt spoke these words after waking up from a sleep he thought was his last. Prueitt, a terminal cancer patient, ingested barbiturates in January 2005 in accordance with Oregon's Death with Dignity Act. He was the first person to live among all those who had ingested legal lethal prescriptions.[464] Two weeks later, he died of natural causes. Since that time, four other individuals have regained consciousness after ingesting legal lethal prescriptions.[465]

Dr. Mel Kohn, Chief Epidemiologist for the Oregon Department of Health Services (DHS), could not explain why Prueitt lived after taking a lethal prescription.[466] Coombs Lee asked him to investigate further.[467] N. Greg Hamilton of Physicians for Compassionate Care compared this to the "the fox offering to investigate the break-in at the chicken house."[468] Prueitt's story is subject to different interpretations, the most plausible of which is that humans have a wide range of responses when administered any drug.

This chapter reviews studies by Drs. Linda Ganzini and Susan Tolle, as well as the *2011 Summary of Oregon's Death with Dignity Act Annual Report.* These studies provide scientific evidence to evaluate the effectiveness of Oregon's law. Ganzini developed a character profile of those who hastened their deaths in the first study.

Physicians' Perceptions of Patients Who Request Assisted Suicide

Dr. Linda Ganzini and her associates at the Oregon Health & Science University reportedß face-to-face interviews with thirty-five Oregon physicians who received a request for lethal prescriptions in the *Journal of Palliative Medicine*.[469] The physicians described patients who requested legal lethal prescriptions as strong-minded individuals who feared loss of independence and accepted death without denial.[470]

One physician remembered a patient who surprised his wife when he told her that he wanted to hasten his death. The woman told her husband that after fifty years of marriage, she should have something to say about the matter. After a serious discussion with her husband, she told the physician, "I think he's right and I support him."[471]

Ganzini suggests that some patients respond more readily to frank, open discussions than to a warm, caring atmosphere. Further research by Ganzini puts the deaths of people who die by legal lethal prescriptions into context.

Patients Who Refuse Food and Fluids to Hasten Death

Many physicians consider death by voluntary refusal of food and drink gruesome, whereas others believe it is a normal process.[472] Ganzini argued that her survey would change minds on both accounts.[473] She mailed a questionnaire to all nurses employed by hospice programs in Oregon, seeking information about patients who died after refusing food and water and those who died after ingesting legal lethal prescriptions. She reported her results in an article in the July 2004 edition of the *New England Journal of Medicine*.[474] Forty-one percent of the 307 hospice nurses who returned the survey reported on patients who chose to stop eating and drinking. Eighteen percent reported on patients who died from legal lethal prescriptions.

This survey indicated that twice as many people died by voluntary refusal of food and fluids than those who died by legal lethal prescription. Those who died by refusing to eat or drink were slightly older (74), suffered from a prolonged neurological disease, did not have a mental health examination, and were resigned to death. Those who died by legal lethal prescription were younger (70), suffered from cancer, had a mental health examination, and expressed a desire to control the circumstances of their death.[475]

Those who died by voluntarily refusing food and water listed the following reasons for their decision: ready to die, poor quality of life, and continued existence seen as pointless. The lowest level of responses for this group was a perception of self as a financial drain on others and having witnessed bad deaths.

Hospice nurses rated the last two weeks of life for these patients as peaceful, with low levels of pain.

Ganzini warned readers that it was impossible to compare peacefulness in dying because of the small number of cases surveyed. Nurses rated patients for peacefulness on a scale that ran from 1 to 10, with 10 the most peaceful. The range for those dying for refusing food and fluids was 7–9, and the range for those dying by legal prescriptions was 6–9.[476]

Langlois of the *Catholic Sentinel* ignored Ganzini's caution. He insisted that her survey proved that patients who stopped eating and drinking died more peaceably than those who died by assisted suicide.[477] Hamilton argued that Ganzini's study compared "apples and oranges."[478] However, a subsequent survey by Tolle confirmed Ganzini's conclusions.

Characteristics of Dying Oregonians Who Consider Physician-Assisted Suicide

Dr. Susan Tolle, director of the Center for Ethics in Health Care at the Oregon Health & Science University, conducted 1,384 telephone interviews of family caregivers of terminal patients. She reported their findings in the August 2004 issue of the *Journal of Clinical Ethics*.[479] Tolle's survey indicated that 17 percent of terminally ill patients considered hastening their deaths, 2 percent requested a lethal prescription, and one in a thousand ingested a lethal prescription.

The study confirmed that more people consider hastened death than follow through with it. These people were younger and better educated than the average Oregonian who died of natural causes. Most of them listed their race as White. They requested lethal prescriptions because of decreased quality of life, loss of autonomy, and high levels of pain.[480]

Family caregivers reported that 44 percent of their loved ones favored hastened death, 42 percent opposed it, and 15 percent were undecided. Tolle observed that Protestants and Catholics were half as likely to favor Death with Dignity as people with no religious affiliation. She concluded that seven years of results had not changed the minds of patients and their families about Oregon's law. She found no slippery slope or evidence of illegality.[481] She presented evidence from a national survey of physicians that the death rate from legal hastened deaths was far less in Oregon than the rate in other states, where such acts are illegal.[482]

Opponents of the Death with Dignity Act criticized Tolle's survey. Hamilton called it "bogus."[483] Langlois insisted that the survey proved that caregivers who discussed options with their loved ones pressured them to take their own lives.[484]

Dr. Margaret Battin, a professor at the University of Utah, confirmed Tolle's conclusions.[485] Ganzini and Dr. Steven K. Dobscha observed in *The Journal of Clinical Ethics* that patients with a tough, independent personality were more likely to bring up the topic of hastened death with their physicians. Those with a higher education were better prepared to surmount the legal safeguards of the Death with Dignity Act. People with control issues often reacted negatively to suggestions that healthcare professionals would take good care of them.[486]

Prevalence of Depression and Anxiety in Patients Requesting Physicians' Aid in Dying

Opponents of Oregon's law believed Ganzini's study provided evidence that made it "too easy for depressed patients to seek a life-ending pill—and too easy for a doctor to prescribe one."[487] This interpretation became an issue in the November 2008 initiative campaign over the Washington Death with Dignity Act, but had little effect on the outcome of the election.

Dr. Linda Ganzini's study, published in the *British Medical Journal*, measured depression and anxiety in terminal patients. She used three standardized psychological tests: Beck's Hopelessness scale, the Hospital Anxiety and Depression scale, and the current mood disorder section of the structured clinical interview for American Psychiatric Association Diagnostic and Statistical Manual-IV axis disorder (SCID-I).

Compassion & Choices of Oregon provided her with the names of forty-seven terminal patients. Ethics consultants, palliative medicine, and oncology specialists referred eleven individuals for a total of fifty-eight. They suffered from cancer (N=44) or ALS (N=7). All requested aid in dying from a physician or advocacy group. Ganzini determined they were capable of consenting to research.[488]

Forty-eight percent of the subjects met the criteria for clinical depression or anxiety on one of the three tests. Eighteen participants received legal lethal prescriptions. Of this number, nine self-administered the prescription and died. Three of those nine met the criteria for clinical depression or anxiety. Ganzini noted the patients who received legal lethal prescriptions had lower depression and hopelessness scores than those who did not but suggested a need for increased vigilance and systematic evaluation on the part of the attending physicians.[489]

Coombs Lee criticized Ganzini's study. "The researchers classified some of the patients as 'depressed,' but sadness and anxiety is to be expected in dying patients."[490] Lee noted that tests designed for healthy persons are inappropriate for assessing the mental state of terminal patients. An analysis of the psychological tests used by Ganzini confirms Coombs Lee's criticisms.

The Beck Hopelessness scale has had no psychometric assessment since its development in 1974.[491] One of the subjects declined to complete it because "she had trouble with the entire concept of hope."[492] A. S. Zigmond and R. P. Snaith developed The Hospital Anxiety and Depression scale in 1982 for patients in outpatient clinics. A key question asks patients if they have thought about death. It is reasonable to believe that terminal patients think about their imminent demise. Psychiatrists designed the SCID-I to screen a normal population for dissociative disorders.[493] It presumes clinically depressed patients have a mental disorder—an inappropriate assumption for terminal patients.[494]

Ganzini's study points out the need for caution on the part of prescribing physicians and the importance of developing psychological tests suited for terminally ill patients, but she found no abuse. Oregon's law rests on the determination of two physicians that the terminal patient is competent to make an informed decision. Depression is a factor only if it renders a patient incompetent. The best way for individuals to make up their minds about Oregon's Act is to look at the evidence collected by the Oregon Department of Human Services.

Annual Report on Oregon's Death with Dignity Act

The Oregon Department of Human Services released the *2011 Summary of Oregon's Death with Dignity Act* based on paperwork and death certificates received as of 29 February 2012. A spokesperson for the Oregon DHS emphasized the department's neutral role in the debate and the need for accurate data in making informed, ethical, and legal decisions.[495]

There were seventeen more deaths in 2011 than in 2010.[496] Physicians wrote six more lethal prescriptions, but the rest of the patterns remained essentially the same. The total number of prescriptions and the number of deaths has slowly risen since the law went into effect. The annual report confirmed studies by Ganzini and Tolle. Many people obtained prescriptions but chose not to take them. Several indicated that they felt reassured, having a lethal prescription in their refrigerators, even if they never used it.[497] Twenty-five of the 114 patients who received prescriptions in 2011 did not take the medication and died of underlying illness.[498]

The report indicated that sixty-two physicians wrote 114 lethal prescriptions. Seventy-one patients took the medications. This included nine patients with prescriptions written in earlier years. This corresponded to 22.5 deaths per 10,000 deaths. The Oregon Medical Board received no referrals for failure to comply with the requirements of the act.

Table 10.1 Prescriptions and Deaths[499]

Year	1998	1999	2000	2001	2002	2003	2004	2005	2006	2007	2008	2009	2010	2011	Total
Rx	24	33	39	44	58	60	60	64	65	85	88	95	96	114	933
Deaths	16	27	27	21	38	42	37	38	46	49	54	53	65	71	596

A profile of the people who hastened their deaths from 1998 through 2011 includes the following: a median age of seventy-one, White (97.6%), male (51.7%), married (45.7%), and dying of cancer (80.9%). Those who took advantage of Oregon's law were better educated than other Oregonians who died of the same diseases. Forty-four percent had a baccalaureate or higher. Most (89.7%) received hospice care, and only eight (1.1%) had no insurance.[500]

Patients' end-of-life concerns have remained constant over fourteen years. The report addresses the fears of foes of the law that hastened death would adversely affect minorities and those without insurance who might seek death to avoid unwanted financial implications or becoming a burden on their families. [501]

Table 10.2 End-of-Life Concerns (N=596)[502]

90.9%	losing autonomy
88.3%	decreasing ability to participate in activities that make life enjoyable
82.7%	loss of dignity
53.7%	losing control of bodily functions
36.1%	burden on family, friends, or caregivers
22.6%	inadequate pain control
2.5%	financial implications of treatment

The Physicians for Compassionate Care Education charged that the DHS report was incomplete and that only one of the seventy-one individuals who died had a psychological referral. They commented, "Are we failing to recognize and address the despair that is frequently found in patients near the end of life?" [503] They noted that the report mentioned two individuals who regurgitated the lethal medication, regained consciousness, and died later from their underlying ailments. They stated, "These are not easy drugs to take, they are bitter and foul-tasting, and vomiting does occur despite anti-emetics." [504]

Over the years, opponents of the Death with Dignity Act insisted that the annual report was "plagued with shortcomings." [505] Kenneth Stevens of Physicians for Compassionate Care insisted the report was biased in methodology and language. [506] He doubted that physicians affiliated with Compassion & Choices, "a death-promoting organization," provided accurate information. [507] He charged that Coombs Lee and Eighmey forced the Oregon Department of Human Services to replace the term "physician-assisted suicide" on their web site with euphemisms as part of a campaign to spread Oregon's law to other states. [508]

Fourteen years of reports and scientific studies indicated that the notion of "fatally flawed" was a myth. There were no seizures or agonizing deaths. The median number of minutes from self-administered ingestion of the lethal prescription to unconsciousness was five minutes. [509]

Tolle noted that terminal patients often asked their physicians about their options under the law.[510] This created an opportunity for medical providers to discuss the fears and wishes of patients. Physicians responded to this opportunity, improved their knowledge of palliative care, and enhanced their skills in recognizing depression.[511]

Conclusion

Ganzini painted a striking picture of the strong-minded individuals who chose hastened death. She compared them to people who died by refusing food and water in a second survey and found that both groups sought dignified deaths with the means available to them. Her latest survey pointed out the need for "increased vigilance and systematic examination for depression" of patients seeking legal lethal prescriptions.[512] Tolle's work indicated that the dying in Oregon discussed options with their loved ones, no slippery slope existed, and physicians who wrote lethal prescriptions did so according to the law.

Proponents and opponents of Oregon's law interpret the evidence in Oregon's annual report in different ways. However, the Vermont Legislative Council Report on "Oregon's Death with Dignity Law and Euthanasia in the Netherlands: Factual Disputes" substantiated these findings, as have many other reports and studies.[513] Dr. Katrina Hedburg, an epidemiologist with the DHS, observed that, "There really isn't much new here. That doesn't mean it won't be controversial for some people."[514]

Dr. Kenneth Stevens of Physicians for Compassionate care said, "I was taught that a prescription is an order from the doctor to the patient. [In assisted death] you're not pulling the trigger, but you're giving the patient a loaded gun."[515] For this reason, those who oppose Oregon's law question surveys and reports with vigor and determination, with the notable exception of Ganzini's cross sectional survey, "Prevalence of Depression and Anxiety in Patients Requesting Physicians' Aid in Dying."

Ann Jackson, head of the Oregon Hospice Association, opposed the Death with Dignity Act in 1994. She now cooperates fully with right-to-die groups.[516] The works of Ganzini and Tolle reinforce the findings of the Oregon DHS. These studies and reports present the data in an easy-to-understand format. People should make up their own minds after considering the scientific evidence and make an informed moral and ethical decision.

A Matter of Conscience:
Life and Death

Conclusion

I started writing about the Death with Dignity Act as a result of my class-room experience. Students couldn't see beyond the rhetoric of their position when the topic concerned abortion, but they spoke from their hearts when the conversation turned to issues at the end of life. This experience gave me some notion of the power of the topic, but only a glimmer of where the controversy would take me. What I knew was that I admired the perseverance of both sides and wanted to objectively analyze their actions and arguments.

The challenge in writing about the Oregon Death with Dignity Act lies in examining a series of events occurring over a prolonged period of time. Barbara Nelson's organizational theory of agenda setting solved this difficulty. She divided issue maintenance into three parts. Initial maintenance is the work one needs to do to establish a policy in good working order. Recurring maintenance is the effort one must expend to preserve it. Successive adoption occurs when other states adopt a policy.

Part I: Initial maintenance began with Elven Sinnard. The death of his wife troubled him deeply. He didn't want others to die alone, so he formed a group that wrote a ballot measure and put it before Oregon voters in 1994. The measure allowed qualified patients to legally hasten their deaths. After a bitter campaign, the voters of Oregon narrowly approved the Death with Dignity Act. Opponents of the law secured a Federal District Court injunction that blocked implementation of the Act.

The members of the Oregon Legislative Assembly debated whether to amend the Death with Dignity Act or refer it back to the people in 1997. Social conservatives characterized the Act as a step toward euthanasia such as was practiced in Nazi Germany.[517] The Republican majority voted to refer the law back to the people. Opponents of the law waged a feisty campaign in the subsequent election. However, the voters of Oregon resented the interference of the legislature and passed the Death with Dignity Act by an overwhelming margin.

That same year the US Supreme Court ruled in *Washington v. Glucksberg* that, although there was no individual right to die, states were free to pass legislation in accordance with the wishes of their citizens. Based on this decision, the Ninth US Circuit Court of Appeals lifted the injunction against the Death with Dignity Act.

Part II: Defenders of Oregon's law fended off attacks upon the Act during recurring maintenance. Senator Wyden blocked legislation in Congress that would have sabotaged Oregon's law. As a result, opponents beseeched the Bush administration for help. Attorney General Ashcroft issued a memorandum that forbade the use of controlled substances to hasten death. Supporters of Oregon's law brought suit against Ashcroft's memorandum and won favorable decisions in Federal District Court and the Ninth Circuit Court of Appeals. Ashcroft appealed these decisions to the US Supreme Court.

A majority of the court ruled on behalf of the state of Oregon in January 2006. This ruling constituted a substantive decision point in the cultural war over the Death with Dignity Act. The Act now rests solidly on two Supreme Court decisions, *Washington v. Glucksberg* and *Gonzales v. Oregon*. The first authorizes states to pass such laws. The second sanctions the use of controlled substances to hasten death for qualified terminal patients. Alice Rutter, a friend and counselor, attended the deaths of six people who chose to legally end their lives. She noted that the Supreme Court ruling "will bring comfort to terminally ill patients who know they have the option if they need it."[518]

Part III: Right-to-life advocates defeated Death with Dignity initiatives in Michigan and Maine. Failure in two Oregon elections taught them the importance of funding and organization. They defeated bills in the legislatures of Hawaii (2002), California (2006), and Vermont (2006).[519] Success lay in controlling the language of the debate and mobilizing public opinion. Right-to-die supporters had a difficult time overcoming right-to-life support in these legislatures and responding to conflicting interpretations of the record in Oregon.

Washington and Montana legalized Death with Dignity eleven years after Oregon's law went into effect. Right-to-die advocates ran a well-financed professional campaign that capitalized on their strengths. They controlled the media battle and responded quickly and effectively to the charges of their opponents.

The work of Kathryn Tucker brought results in Montana. Opponents of Death with Dignity lost an appeal to the State Supreme Court and failed to pass bills in the legislature outlawing hastened death. Opponents would like to take the battle back to Congress, but it is not likely in the foreseeable future. The Supreme Court decided in *Gonzales v. Oregon* (2006) that states had a right to pass legislation similar to Oregon's law. Senator Gordon Smith (R-OR) accepted the Court's ruling as final and suggested that Congress do the same.[520]

The opponents of Death with Dignity believe the core values of Western civilization are at stake. They are clad in the armor of moral conviction. These setbacks have increased their ardor. They believe the right-to-die movement has gained momentum. They will scrutinize every shred of evidence from surveys and reports, consider the lessons they have learned, and anticipate their enemy's next move. Dr. Charles Bentz, president of Physicians for Compassionate care cautioned his supporters, "Don't take everything the proponents say at face value. Question their assumptions and data."[521] Pro-life supporters do not see other states adopting such legislation in the near future.[522]

As the right-to-die movement considers legislation and legal challenges in states less favorable to their cause, the balance of forces will shift to their opponents. Representative Earl Blumenauer (D-OR) recognized the energy and ingenuity of social conservatives, observing, "I hope that whatever they do, they leave us alone, and I hope they take a deep breath and consider what the public wants."[523]

On a brighter note, palliative care has improved. Valerie Vollmar, a professor at Willamette University College of Law and author of an extensive website on physician-assisted death, noted that both supporters and opponents of Death with Dignity laws advocate increasing the availability of hospice care and improving pain management for the dying. She noted that as a result, "End-of-life care in Oregon has improved dramatically."[524]

Attitudes change when people talk about death. People in states where such discussions have occurred are more aware of the need of advance directives, pain control management, and hospice care. The debate over Death with Dignity laws in other states will have far-reaching consequences. Some states will permit hastened death. Others will not.

I interviewed a number of people in my research for this book. They helped me analyze how issues inspire individuals and motivate organizations. Their personal stories illustrated the difficulties inherent in making decisions at the end of life. I hope the people that I conversed with understand that, even though my heart goes out to them, my craft as a political scientist dictates a nonjudgmental approach to the subject. Political science focuses on the mechanics of how governments allocate values. Religion focuses on the ethical dimension of those values.

Supreme Court Judge Kennedy correctly described *Gonzales v. Oregon* as a "hard case."[525] Although my professional views on the issue are much clearer, my personal views remain as conflicted today as when I first discussed the issue with my wife. Oregon's Death with Dignity Act fostered a nationwide debate. However, most Americans examine their beliefs and the dictates of the situation when faced with the death of a loved one. Each individual's conscience remains the site of the final battlefield.

Works Cited

"Ad Campaign to Fight Proposal B." *The Michigan Daily* 15 Aug. 1998. <http://www.pub.umich.edu/daily/1998/sep/09-15-98> Accessed 28 July 2007.

Advertisement. *Honolulu Advertiser* PDF file. HPACC Website. <www.hpacc.org> Accessed 28 Dec. 2010.

American Civil Liberties Union. Andrew Frey counsel of record. *Gonzales v. Oregon* 64-623 in the Supreme Court of the United States in support of the respondents, 18 July 2005: 22.

Angell, Kenneth. Statement on Vermont "Death with Dignity." Proposal. 30 Jan. 2003.

Angell, Marcia. "Keep Alive the Right to Die." *Mail Tribune* 5 Oct. 2005: 5B.

"2009 Annual PAS Report Press Release." Physicians for Compassionate Care Education Foundation. 4 Mar. 2010.

Arakawa, Lynda, and Kevin Dayton. "Assisted Suicide Rejected." *Honolulu Advertiser* 3 May 2002. <http//the.honoluluadvertiser.com> Accessed 28 Dec. 2012.

Ashcroft, John. Office of the Attorney General, Washington, D.C. 6 Nov. 2001. Memorandum for Asa Hutchinson, Administrator, Drug Enforcement Administration.

Ashcroft v. Oregon. 04-623, US Supreme Court, Nov. 9, 2004. On Petition for a Writ of Certiorari, 2004 WL 2544622 (U.S.): 1.

Asseo, Laurie. "Court Told Assisted Suicide Is Common." *Oregonian* 11 Dec. 1996: A8.

"Assisted Suicide Vote Will Be on Maine Ballot." CNS News. 20 May 2000: Euthanasia Home Page. <http://www.euthanasia.com> Accessed 28 July 2007.

Autonomy Inc. and Cascade AIDS Project. Amy Sabrin counsel of record. Brief, *Gonzales v. Oregon* 64-623 in the Supreme Court of the United States in support of the respondents, 21 July 2005: 16.

"Background Check." *Oregonian* 31 Mar. 2005: A8.

Bagwell, Jennifer. "The Right to Die." *Metro Times* 16 Aug. 1998. <www.Metro-times.com/news/stories/news/18/51/mrnsfds.html> Accessed 27 July 2007.

Balmer, Thomas A. Oregon Assistant Attorney General. Telephone interview. 25 June 2007.

Barber, Sister Francine. Homily at Blessed Theresa of Calcutta Parish, Wood-ville, WA. 12 Oct. 2008. <http://wwwthewccc.org> Accessed 2 Dec. 2008.

Barnett, Erin Hoover. "Activists Turn Inventive to Aid Suicide Option." *Oregon-ian* 12 Nov. 1999: A1.

———. "Dilemma of Assisted Suicide: When?" *Oregonian* 17 Jan. 1999: A1.

———. "A Family Struggle: Is Mom Capable of Choosing to Die?" Part 2, *Oregonian* 17 Oct. 1999: G1.

———. "Is Mom Capable of Choosing to Die?" Part 1, *Oregonian* 16 October 1999: G1.

Barnett, Erin Hoover, and Ashbel S. Green. "Assisted-Suicide Law Faces New Challenges in Court, Congress." *Oregonian* 12 July 1998: A1.

———. "The Reaction: State Officials and Doctors Will Challenge the Action." *Oregonian* 7 Nov. 2001: A15.

Barnett, Erin Hoover, and Dave Hogan. "Assisted Suicide Again Targeted." *Ore-gonian* 11 June 1999: C1.

Barnett, Jim. "Court: Justices Fire Questions at Both Sides." *Oregonian* 6 Oct 2005: A1.

———. "The Insider and the Gadfly." *Oregonian* 23 April 2000: D1.

———. "Judge's Federal Stance May Favor Suicide Law." *Oregonian* 21 July 2005: A1.

———. "Oregon Assisted Suicide Law Hangs on Tax Bill." *Oregonian* 26 Oct. 2000: A1.

———. "Senator Smith Ends Opposition to State's Law in Light of Ruling." *Oregonian* 18 Jan. 2006: 1A.

———. "State Suicide Law Waits on Bush." *Oregonian* 11 June 2001: E8.

———. "Suicide Law Survives One Challenge But Faces Another." *Oregonian* 16 Dec. 2000: A1.

Barnett, Jim, and Dave Hogan. "House Panel Votes to Block Suicide Law." *Oregonian* 5 Aug. 1998: AI.

———. "Measure to Block Assisted Suicide Appears Sidelined." *Oregonian* 7 Oct. 1998: AI.

———. "Senate Oks Giving Rural Oregon $115 Million." *Oregonian* 7 Oct. 2000. <http://www.oregonlive.com/special/assisted_suicide/index.ssf?/news> Accessed 28 Dec. 2006.

———. "Suicide Bill Feud Grows Intense." *Oregonian* 6 May 2000: AII.

———. Wyden Halts Vote on Suicide Bill." *Oregonian* 30 Oct. 2000: EI.

Barnett, Jim, and Jeff Kosseff. "Oregon Law Uncertain as 'Culture' Strengthens." *Oregonian* 27 Mar. 2005: AI.

———. "Schiavo Case Puts New Focus on Oregon." *Oregonian* 27 Mar. 2005: AI.

Bates, Tom. "Elven O. Sinnard." *Oregonian* 2 Feb. 1997: BI.

———. "Senator Drops Effort to Block Suicide Law." *Oregonian* 15 Oct. 1998: AI.

———. "Suicide Injunction Stands." *Oregonian* 24 April 1996: CI.

———. "Vatican Article Denounces State's Assisted Suicide." *Oregonian* I Dec. 1994: A23.

———. "Write to Die." *Oregonian* 18 Dec. 1994: AI.

Bates, Tom, and Mark O'Keefe. "Oregon Is a Maverick." *Oregonian* 13 Nov. 1994: AI.

Baxter, Robert. Affidavit for the Montana First Judicial District Court, *Baxter et al v. Montana*, 28 June 2008: 3.

Baxter et al v. Montana. 5 Dec. 2008. Decision and Order: 15.

Benson, Arden R. Letter. *Oregonian* 26 Oct. 1997: E5.

Bentz, Charles. E-mail to author. "Get Involved." From Physicians for Compassionate Care, 15 Oct. 2008.

"Beyond Red and Blue." Pew Research Center. <http.www.people-press.org> Accessed 27 Dec. 2006.

"Bishop Pledges to Fight Ruling Legalizing Assisted Suicide in Montana." *The Pilot* 9 Jan. 2009: 7.

Borreca, Richard. "Assisted Suicide Measure Could Die Early in Senate." *Honolulu Star Bulletin* I Mar 2002. <http//starbulletin.com> Accessed 28 Dec. 2006.

Bradbury, Bill. *Oregon Blue Book, 2005-2006.* Portland Daily Journal of Commerce, 2005.

Brandt-Erichsen, David. *Congress Daily* 25 Sep. 1998. <www.cryonet.org> Accessed 13 March 2012.

Brief Amicus Curiae of the American Hospital Association. *Washington v. Glucksberg* <http://uphs.upenn.edu/-bioethic/PAS/Sa.html> Accessed 27 Dec. 2006.

Brief, Amicus Curiae of Senators and Representatives. *Gonzales v. Oregon*, 64-623 in the Supreme Court, 11 May 2005: 2.

Brief for the Patient-Respondents. Nicholas van Aelstyn, counsel of record, and Kathryn Tucker, Compassion & Choices. *Gonzales v. Oregon* 64-623 in the Supreme Court of the United States in support of the respondents, 10 Jan. 2005.

Brief of the Petitioners. Paul Clement, Acting Attorney General et al. *Gonzales v. Oregon* 64-623 in the Supreme Court of the United States, 2 Feb. 2004: iii.

Brief for Respondent State of Oregon, Hardy Myers et al. *Gonzales v. Oregon* 64-623 in the Supreme Court of the United States in support of the respondents, 18 July 2005: 21

Brief for Respondents, State of Oregon et al., filed by Peter Rasmussen and David Hochhalter, Eli Stutsman counsel of record, 21 July 2005.

Briggs, David. "Bishops Attack Assisted Suicide." *Oregonian* 18 Nov. 1994: A23.

Brislin, Richard. "Culture Clash." *Star-Bulletin* 2 June 2002. <http//starbulletin. com/2002/06/02/business/brislin.html> Accessed 28 Dec. 2006.

Broder, David. *Democracy Derailed.* New York: Harcourt Inc., 2000.

Brooks, Francis. Vermont Sergeant at Arms. Personal interview. 19 July 2007.

"Brownback Should Butt Out." Editorial. *Mail Tribune* 18 August 2006: 5B.

Bushong, Stephen K. *Oregon v. Ashcroft,* Outline of Issues and Authorities, Oct. 2002: 5.

"Campaign Watch: Measure 16: Backers Report." *Oregonian* 22 Sept. 1994: C4.

Campbell, Courtney S. "The Oregon Trail to Death: Measure 16—Euthanasia Initiative." *Commonweal* 19 August 1994. <http://findarticles.com> Accessed 18 May 2007.

Carson, Teresa. "Schiavo Case Casts Spotlight on Oregon Suicide Law." *Reuters*, 22 Mar. 2005. <http://www.alertnet.org/aenews/newsdesk> Accessed 28 Dec. 2006.

Catholic Medical Association. Teresa Collett. Brief Amicus Curiae, *Gonzales v. Oregon* 64-623 in the Supreme Court of the United States in Support of petitioners and in Support of Reversal, 11 May 2005: 2.

"Challenges in Court, Congress." *Oregonian* 12 July 1998: A1.

Christie, Tim. "Oregon Suicide Law Comes to High Court." *Register-Guard* 4 Oct. 2005: 1.

CNN News Exit Poll I-1000. Election 2008. 24 Nov. 2008. <http://www.cnn.com/ELECTION/2008/results/polls/#WAI01pl.> Accessed 9 Jan 2009

Colburn, Don. "Ailing Man Caught in Legal Limbo." *Oregonian* 8 Nov. 2001: A1.

———. "Assisted-Suicide Attempt Fails." *Oregonian* 4 Mar. 2005: A1.

———. "Assisted Suicides Increase." *Oregonian* 19 Mar. 2008: E1.

———. "Doctor-Assisted Suicide Cases Flat in 2005." *Oregonian* 10 March 2006: D1.

———. "End-of-Life Debate Starts Earlier, Goes Differently in Oregon." *Oregonian* 27 Mar. 2005: A1.

———. "Fewer Turn to Assisted Suicide." *Oregonian* 11 March 2005: A1.

———. "A Moment of Triumph." *Oregonian* 18 Jan. 2006: A8.

———. "Oregon Activists Tell Washington What to Expect." *Oregonian* 10 Jan. 2008. <http:/www/lexisnexis.com.proxy.tui.edu/us/Inacademic/frame> Accessed 12 Sep. 2008.

———. "Other States See Path." *Oregonian* 22 Jan. 2006: A1.

———. "Washington's Death with Dignity Isn't a Trend: Opponents and Supporters Say." *Oregonian* 7 Nov. 2008. <http://oregonlivelcom> Accessed 14 Dec. 2008.

———. "Why Am I Not Dead?" *Oregonian* 4 Mar. 2005: A1.

———. "25% of Sick Who Choose Suicide May Be Depressed." *Oregonian* 8 Oct. 2008: A1.

Collins, Paul M. "Lobbyists Before the U.S. Supreme Court." *Political Research Quarterly* 69 (1 March 2007): 65.

"Come-from-Behind Victory Against Maine Assisting Suicide Referendum Elates Anti Euthanasia Forces." National Right to Life Committee. 24 July 2000 <http:www.nrlc.org/nes/2000/NRL12/maine.html> Accessed 29 July 2007.

"Compassion & End-of-Life Choices." *Connections* 12.1 (Spring 2004): 6.

Compassion in Dying v. Washington. 1994, United States District Court for the Western District of Washington, Seattle Division, 850 F. Supp. 1454.

Compassion in Dying v. Washington. 1996, Ninth US Circuit Court of Appeals, 79 F, 3d 790: 1196 US App.

Compassion in Dying v. Washington. 1996. Ninth Circuit Court of Appeals, 79 F3d (en banc). 850 F. Supp. at 1455–57.

"Congress Threatens to Repeal DWD Act." *The Compassion Report* 3.3 (Fall/ Winter 2000): 1.

Congressional Record. 27 Sep. 1998: S10883 (DOCID:cr24se98-141).

Congressional Record. 14 Oct. 1998: S12491 (DOCI:cr14oct98-199).

Congressional Record. 26 Oct. 2000: S11104 (DOCIS:cr260c00pt2-63).

Consejo, Michel. Vermont State Representative. Personal interview. 19 Jan. 2007.

Constantine, Thomas A. Letter from DEA administrator to Representative Henry Hyde, 5 Nov. 1997.

Corneliussen, Amy. "Controversial Judge Dismisses Detractors." *Corvallis Gazette Times* 19 Jan. 1998: 1.

"Court Confuses Liberty, Death." Editorial. *Oregonian* 4 Mar. 1996: C8.

"Court Hears Case for Assisted Suicide." *Oregonian* 27 Oct. 1995: C11.

Daly, Mathew. "Wyden to Fight for Assisted Suicide Law." *Mail Tribune* 6 Sep. 2006: 1A.

Davis, Jim. State of Oregon, Voters' Pamphlet, Statewide Measures 4 Nov. 1994.

Davis, Adam, and Tim Hibbitts. Oregon Statewide Poll Conducted by Market Decisions Corporation for the *Oregonian* Sep. 1997.

"Death by Dehydration Seems Peaceful, Nurses Say." *Reuters.* 24 July 2003. <http://www.wllspan.org/Health/News/reuters/NewsStory0724200313.htm> Accessed 28 Dec. 2006.

"The Death with Dignity Alliance." *Connections.* Published by Compassion in Dying Federation, (Summer 2002): 7.

"Death with Dignity, Approve I-1000." Editorial. *Seattle Times* 8 Oct 2008. <http://seattletimes.nwsource.com> Accessed 26 Nov. 2008.

Death with Dignity Facts Website. Northwest Passage Counseling. n.d. <deathwithdignityfacts.com/default.aspx?ID=35> Accessed 26 Nov. 2008.

The Death with Dignity Report. (Fall 2008): 1.

"Death Without Dignity." Editorial. *Oregonian* 11 May 1997: E4.

Death with Dignity National Center. "Efforts in Michigan." 17 Feb. 2006. <www.deathwithdignity.org/news/news/michigan.asd> Accessed 28 July 2007.

Department of Health Services News Release, 9 Mar. 2004. http://www/ dhs.state.or.us/news/2004news/2004-0309a.html> Accessed 9 Nov. 2007.

Detzel, Tom, and Jim Barnett. "Wyden to Bush: Keep Hands Off Suicide Law." *Oregonian* 31 Oct. 2001: DI.

"Did Chief Justice Roberts Mislead Senator Wyden?" Blue Oregon. Open discussion. <www://blueoregon.com/2006/01/drd_Chief_Justi.html> Accessed 28 Dec. 2006.

Dinan, John. "Rights and the Political Process: Physician-Assisted Suicide in the Aftermath of Washington v. Glucksberg." *Publius: The Journal of Federalism* 31.4 (2001): 1-22.

Dionne, E. J. "Lively Debate on Dying." *Oregonian* 30 June 1997: B12.

"Disability Activists Criticize Administration." PRWeb, press release newswire 18 Jan. 2006. <http://www/prweb.com/Releases/2006/1/prwieb224213.html> Accessed 28 Dec. 2006.

"Doctor-Daughter." YouTube 14 Oct. 2008 <http://www.youtube.com/ watch?v=LjgBIyJuXI> Accessed 28 Nov. 2008.

"Don't Bully Oregon." Editorial. *Oregonian* 9 May 2000: D12.

Duin, Steve. "His Conscience Provides Solace Only for One." *Oregonian* April 30, 2000: DI.

———. "Kate Cheney Still Doesn't Rest in Peace." *Oregonian* 11 Nov. 1999: CI.

———. "Votin', Gloatin' Pioneers." *Oregonian* 9 Nov. 1997: BI.

Duntley, Mark. "Moral Authority and Assisted Suicide." *Sojourners: Christians for Justice and Peace* (May–June), 1995.

Durbin, Kathie. "Out-of-State Interests Spend Big on I-1000." *The Columbian* 28 Aug. 2008: A1.

Editorial. "Protect the Dying." *Oregonian* 5 Aug. 1995: D4.

Egan, Timothy, and Adam Liptak. "Fraught Issue, Narrow Ruling." *New York Times* 18 Jan. 2006: A16.

Eighmey, George. E-mail to author. 22 May 2004 and 19 Nov. 2008.

———. "Executive Director's Page." Compassion & Choices of Oregon Newsletter. Dec. 2006: 2.

———. Executive Director Oregon Compassion & Choices. Personal interview. 13 August 2007.

———. "Study Finds Dying Patients Think About Death." Compassion & Choices, October 2008.

"Elven 'Al' Sinnard Dies." Compassion in Dying Newsletter, 8.1 (Spring 2000): 3.

Ertedt, Steven. "California Bill Would Legalize Assisted Suicide." *LifeNews.com* 9 Nov. 2004: 1.

———. "Washington Former Governor Will Still Head Up Assisted Suicide Bill." *LifeNews* 17 Oct. 2008. <http://www.lifenews.com/bio1805.html> Accessed 26 Nov. 2008.

Fischer, Mary A. "To Live or Die." *Readers Digest* 3 May 2003. <http/www.deathwithdignity.org/resources/articles.readers_digest> Accessed 29 Dec. 2006.

Fitzhenry, Robert. *The Harper Book of Quotations*. New York: HarperPerenial, 1993.

Flowers, Janet. Oregon State Elections Division. E-mails to author. 12 and 18 June 2007.

Fogarty, Colin. "Appeals Court Upholds Death with Dignity Act." Oregon Public Broadcasting, 26 May 2004.

Folmar, Kate. "Californians Favor Assisted Suicide." *Mercury News* 2 Mar. 2005. <MercuryNews.com> Accessed 28 Dec. 2006.

Frankham, Jonquil. "New Washington No On I-1000 Ad Features Woman Who Was Offered Assisted Suicide by Insurance Company." LifeStyleNews.com. 28 Oct. 2008. <http://groupsyahoo.com/group/private/message> Accessed 15 July 2009.

Gafke, Roger, and David Leuthold. "The Effect on Voters of Misleading, and Difficult Ballot Titles." *Public Opinion Quarterly* 43.3 (Autumn 1979): 394-401.

Ganzini. Linda, "Prevalence of Depression and Anxiety in Patients Requesting Physicians' Aid in Dying: Cross Sectional Survey." *British Medical Journal* (2008): 337: a1682.

Ganzini, Linda. "Clinical Responses from the Caregivers." Speech Fifth Anniversary Forum: "Results of the Oregon "Experiment." 4 Oct. 2002.

Ganzini, Linda, and Steven K. Dobscha. "Clarifying Distinctions Between Contemplating and Completing Physician-Assisted Suicide." *The Journal of Clinical Ethics* 15.2 (2004): 119–122.

Ganzini, Linda, Steven Dobscha, Ronald Heintz, and Nancy Press. "Oregon Physicians' Perceptions of Patients Who Request Assisted Suicide and Their Families." *Journal of Palliative Medicine* 6. 3 (2003): 557–563.

Ganzini, Linda, Elizabeth Goy, Lois Miller, Theresa Harvath, Ann Jackson, and Molly Delorit. "Nurses' Experiences with Hospice Patients Who Refuses Food and Fluids to Hasten Death." *New England Journal of Medicine* 349. 4 (24 July 2004): 359–365.

Ganzini, Linda, Heidi Nelson, Melinda Lee, et al. "Oregon Physicians' Attitudes About and Experiences with End-of-Life Care Since the Passage of the Oregon Death with Dignity Act." *Journal of the American Medical Association* 2888 (2002): 91–98.

Ganzini, Linda, Heidi Nelson, Teri Schmidt, Dale Kraemer, Molly Delorit, and Melinda Lee. "Physicians' Experiences with the Oregon Death with Dignity Act." *New England Journal of Medicine* 342.8 (24 Feb. 2000): 557–563.

Garrow, David J. "Nine Justices and a Funeral." *George* (June 1977): 56.

Gonzales v. Oregon, US Supreme Court, October Term 2005, 04-623, Majority Opinion Judge Kennedy: 2.

Gonzales v. Oregon, US Supreme Court, October Term 2005, 04-623, Dissenting Opinion Judge Scalia: 4.

Gonzales v. Oregon, US Supreme Court, October Term 2005, 04-623, Dissenting Opinion Judge Thomas: 60.

Gonzales v. Oregon, US Supreme Court, Oral Arguments before the Court, 5 Oct. 2005.

Goodman, Ellen. "Ashcroft's Assisted Suicide Stance Is Simply Bizarre." *Mail Tribune* 15 Nov. 2001: 8A.

———. "Nation Turns to Oregon." *Oregonian* 8 Nov. 1997: D6.

Goodwin, Peter. Board Directors Oregon Compassion & Choices. Personal interview. 18 June 2007.

Green, Ashbel. "Ashcroft Buttresses Suicide Law Challenge." *Oregonian* 24 Sep. 2002: A1.

———. "Judges Quiz Attorneys on Oregon Assisted Suicide Law." *Oregonian* 8 May 2003: C1.

———. "Ruling Ads Time to Weigh Suicide Law." *Oregonian* 21 Nov. 2001: A1.

———. "State Wins Time to Defend Suicide Law." *Oregonian* 9 Nov. 2001: A1.

———. "Suicide Law Argued Today." *Oregonian* 7 May 2003: A1.

———. "Suicide Law May Go to 9th Circuit." *Oregonian* 21 April 2002: A1.

———. "Suicide Law Returns to Voters." *Oregonian* 10 June 1997: A1.

———. "Suicide Law Upheld." *Oregonian* 18 April 2002: A1.

Green Ashbel, and Jim Barnett. "Assisted Suicide Under Siege in Court and Capitol." *Oregonian* 20 Feb. 2005: A1.

Green, Ashbel, and Don Colburn. "Court Bars Ashcroft Role in Suicide Law." *Oregonian* 27 Mar. 2004: A1.

———. "Justices Back Oregon Suicide Law." *Oregonian* 18 Jan. 2005: A8.

Greenhouse, Linda. "Court, 6-3, Says Attorney General Was Wrong in Oregon Case." *New York Times* 18 Jan. 2006: A16.

Gross, Janet. "Landscape Evolves for Assisted Suicide." *The New York Times* 11 Nov. 2008: Health, 11.

Haines, Deacon Bill, and Gina Haines. Homily at St. Louise de Marillac Church, Bellevue WA, 19 Oct. 2008. <http://wwwthewccc.org.> Accessed 2 Dec. 2008.

Halpern, Roland. E-mail to author. 24 July 2003.

———. Executive Director Hawaii Death with Dignity. Personal interview. 11 June 2003.

———. Letter. "Don't Despair." *Honolulu Advertiser* 12 Mar. 2004. <http//www/r\org/states/Hawaii/news-archives.org> Accessed 28 Dec. 2006.

Hamilton, N. Greg. "Assisted Suicide Puts Patients at Risk." *Washington Times* 29 Sept. 2000.

———. "Assisted Suicide Report Plagued by Shortcomings." Physicians for Compassionate Care Press Release, 23 February 2000: 2.

———. "Bias Makes Travesty of Assisted-Suicide Report." *Oregonian* 7 Feb. 2004: C4.

———. "Hawaii Rejects Assisted Suicide." Press release. 2 May 2002.

———. "Physicians for Compassionate Care on Coos Bay Death." Press release Physicians For Compassionate Care. 11 March 1999.

———. "Physicians for Compassionate Care Reacts to the Ninth Circuit Court of Appeals Decision." Press Release. 25 May 2004: 1.

Harmon, Steve. "Right-to-Die Battle Looks to Be Lengthy." *Contra Costa Times* 7 July 2006 <http://www.deathwithdignity.org> Accessed 30 July 2007.

Hatfield, Mark O. in *Official 1997 Special Election Voters' Guide, State of Oregon.* compiled and distributed by Phil Keisling, Secretary of State: 6.

Hawaii Death with Dignity Act HB2487. House of Representatives, Twenty-first Legislature, 2002, State of Hawaii.

"Heart of the Issue." Editorial. *Mail Tribune* 28 June 2000: 12A.

Heinz, Spencer. "Assisted Suicide: Advocates Weigh In." *Oregonian* 9 Dec. 1994: A1.

Heinz, Spencer, and Mark O'Keefe. "Judge Puts Suicide Law On Hold." *Oregonian* 28 Dec. 1994: A1.

Hendin, Herbert, and Kathleen Foley. *The Case Against Assisted Suicide.* Baltimore: Johns Hopkins University Press, 2002.

Herman, William. "My Life Does Not Belong To The State of Church." Letter. *Seattle Times.* 17 Jan. 2008 <http://seattletimes.nwsource.com> Accessed 26 Nov. 2008.

Hill, Gail Kinsey. "The Ad Wars." *Oregonian* 3 Nov. 1997: A8.

———. "Inside, Not Outside Influences Voters." *Oregonian* 30 Oct. 1997: A1.

———. "Kitzhaber Supports Assisted Suicide." *Oregonian* 3 Aug. 1997: A1.

———. "Kitzhaber Vetoes Assisted-Suicide Ballot Title." *Oregonian* 30 July 1997: E5.

———. "Legislators Discuss Special Session." *Oregonian* 6 Nov. 1997: A1.

———. "Message Same as Vote Nears End." *Oregonian* 1 Nov. 1997: A1.

———. "Oregon Could Set Course on Suicide Debate in U.S." *Oregonian* 25 Sep. 1997: AI.

Hill, Gail, and Ashbel Green. "Initiative Campaigns Wallow in Cash." *Oregonian* 3 Nov. 1994: C7.

Hill, Gail, and Erin Hoover. "Two Die Using Suicide Law." *Oregonian* 26 Mar. 1998: AI.

Hill, Gail Kinsey, and Mark O'Keefe. "Church Follows New Political Path." *Oregonian* 16 Oct. 1997: AI.

Hillyard, Daniel, and John Dombrink. *Dying Right: The Death with Dignity Movement.* New York: Routledge, 2001.

Hoffman, Kathy Barks. "Only Oregon Has Assisted Suicide Law." Associated Press Online, 26 May 2007. <http://wib.lexis-nexis.com.proxy.tui.edu/univers/document> Accessed 17 Sep. 2007.

Hogan, Dave, and Erin Hoover Barnett. "Assisted Suicide Again Targeted." *Oregonian* 11 June 1999: CI.

Hogan, Dave, and Jeff Mapes. "Is Oregon Losing Its Initiative?" *Oregonian* 22 May 2003: AI.

Hoover, Erin. "Suicide: Debate Will Resume in Next Session of Congress." *Oregonian* 15 Oct. 1998: BI.

———. "Suicide Laws Unlikely Elsewhere." *Oregonian* 18 Nov. 1997: AI.

Hoover, Will. "Assisted Suicide Bills Get Hearing." *Honolulu Advertiser* 24 Feb. 2002 <http://the.honoluluadvertiser.com> Accessed 28 Dec. 2006.

Hopcraft, Steve. "Ganzini Depression Study Comment." *Compassion & Choices* 6 Oct. 2008.

Howard, Joseph. "American Bioethics Advisory Committee." <http://all.org/abac/ch00I.htm> Accessed 27 Dec. 2006.

Hughes, John. "House Measure Attacks Suicide Law." *Mail Tribune* 5 Aug. 1998: 5A.

Humphry, Derek. Letter. *New York Times* 3 Dec. 1994: 22.

———. "Perspectives on Assisted Suicide." *Los Angeles Times* 8 Mar. 1996: BII.

I-1000 Vote By County. Washington Secretary of State, 5 Nov. 2008 <http://vote.wa.gov/elections/wei/ResultsByCounty> Accessed 30 Nov. 2008.

In Brief, Press Release, 5 June 1998, US House of Representatives Committee on the Judiciary, Henry J. Hyde, Chairman. <www.house.gov/judiciary/jb0622399html> Accessed 28 Dec. 2006.

"In Congress Nickles Pushes, Wyden Defends." *Connections* 2.1 (Fall 2000): 1.

"Individual Rights Win a Round." Editorial. *The News Register* (McMinnville OR) Reprinted in the *Mail Tribune* 28 Jan. 2006: 4B.

International Task Force on Euthanasia and Assisted Suicide. "Oregon Takes a Closer Look at Assisted Suicide." 11. 4 (1997): 1.

Iwasaki, John. "State Second in Nation to Allow Lethal Prescriptions." *Seattle Post-Intelligencer* 5 Nov. 2008. <http//seattlepi.nwresource.com> Accessed 28 Nov. 2008.

Jay, Susan. "Suicide Law Stands." *Mail Tribune* 1 Nov. 1997: 1.

Jenkins, Austin. "Supporters of Washington Assisted Suicide Decry Catholic Money." Oregon Public Broadcasting Website. 14 Aug. 2008 <http://news.opb.org> Accessed 13 Sep. 2008.

Kardon, Josh. Chief of Staff for Senator Ron Wyden. Telephone interview. 7 Sep. 2007.

Karras, Christy. "Terminally Ill Patients Join Fight." *Mail Tribune* 8 Nov. 2001: 3A.

Keisling, Phil, Compiler and publisher. *Oregon Blue Book,* 1997.

Kettler, Bill. "Death in Family." *Mail Tribune* 25 June 2000: A1.

————. "Joan Lucas Left No Details." *Mail Tribune* 26 June 2000: A1.

"Killing Grandma." Editorial. *Brainstorm Magazine Northwest* Nov. 1999. <http://znetsolutions.com/brainstorm.nsf/614372ec75bbbbc8825678a00e3ed9> Accessed 28 Dec. 2006.

Killen, Patricia, and Mark Shibley. "Surveying the Religious Landscape," *The Pacific Northwest, The None Zone.* Ed. Patricia Killen and Mark Silk, New York: Rowan and Littlefield, 2004.

"Kitzhaber: Keep Measure 16." *Oregonian* 24 July 1997: D1.

Kleffman, Sandy. "Doctor Disciplined Over Pain Treatment." *Contra Costa Times* (Walnut Creek, CA) 17 Jan. 2004: A3.

————. "Suit Filed Over Pain Treatment of Ill Man." *Contra Costa Times* (Walnut Creek, CA) 28 Mar. 2003: A1.

Kokua, Crystal. "Death with Dignity Makes Platform." *Honolulu Star-Bulletin* 3 June 2002. <http://starbulletin.com/2002/06/02/news/story. html> Accessed 28 Dec. 2006.

———. "Senate Kills Death-with-Dignity Bill." *Honolulu Star-Bulletin* 2 June 2002. <http://starbulletin.com> Accessed 28 Dec. 2006.

Kosmin, Bary, and Egon Mayer. *American Religious Identification Survey.* New York: The Graduate Center of the City University of New York, 2001. Exhibit 15.

Kosseff, Jeff. "Wyden Vows Fight on Bid to Ban Assisted Suicide." *Oregonian* 14 Mar. 2005: A1.

Kravets, David. "Feds Go After Assisted-Suicide Law." *Mail Tribune* 24 Sep. 2002: A1.

La Corte, Rachel. "Washingtonians Weigh Assisted Suicide." *Mail Tribune* 15 June 2008: 4B.

Lane, Dee. "Judges' Decision on Measure 16 Stirs Conflicting Views." *Oregonian* 29 Dec. 1994: A7.

Langlois, Ed. "Assisted-Suicide Case Seems Bound for High Court." *Catholic Sentinel* 4 June 2004: 1.

———. "Assisted Suicide Report Plagued by Shortcomings." Physicians for Compassionate Care Press Release, 23 February 2000: 2.

———. "Assisted-Suicide Debate Likely to Move Back to Congress." *Catholic Sentinel* 20 Jan. 2006: 1.

———. "Bias Makes Travesty of Assisted-Suicide Report." *Oregonian* 7 Feb. 2004: C4.

———. "Bishops to File Brief in Assisted-Suicide Case." *Catholic Sentinel* 27 September 2002: 6.

———. "Case Shows Depressed Patients Could Fall Victim to Assisted-Suicide Law." *Catholic Sentinel* 14 May 2004: 1.

———. "Catholic and Pro-Life Groups Hail Ruling to Thwart Assisted Suicide." *Catholic Sentinel* 9 Nov. 2001: A1.

———. "Church Leaders Put Hopes on High Court." *Catholic Sentinel* 18 April 2002: 2.

———. "Dying Oregonians Feel Pressure to Take Their Own Lives, Suicide Study Implies." *Catholic Sentinel* 27 Sept. 2004: 1.

————. "In a Steady Rise, Record Number Used Oregon's Assisted-Suicide Law in 2003." *Catholic Sentinel* 1 Jan. 2004: 1.

————. "Judge's Assisted-Suicide Ruling Set in Context of Grueling Moral Debate." *Catholic Sentinel* 1 Nov. 2001. <http:/209.238.166/Suicide-Nov01.shtml#Nov23_01> Accessed 20 Dec. 2006.

————. "Legislators Bring Suicide Flaws to the Surface." *Catholic Sentinel* 21 Mar. 1997: 1.

————. "Man's Assisted-Suicide Attempt Draws Attention to the Practice's Flaws." *Catholic Sentinel* 11 Mar. 2005: 1.

————. "Medical Marijuana Ruling May Suggest Fate of Oregon's Assisted Suicide Law." *Catholic Sentinel* 25 May 2001: 1.

————. "Patient's Brother-in-Law Helps with Suicide." *Catholic Sentinel* 19 March 1999. <www:sentinel.org/articles/1999-12/2345.htl> Accessed 22 Dec. 2006.

————. "Pro-Euthanasia Oregon Voters Driven by Anger at Legislature." *Catholic Sentinel* 19 Dec. 1997: 1.

————. "Refusal to Eat, Drink at Life's End Not Aimed at Suicide, Health Workers Say." *Catholic Sentinel* 1 Aug. 2003: 1.

————. "Senate Prepares to Take Up Pain Relief Promotion Act." *Catholic Sentinel* 5 Nov. 1999. <http://209,238.223.166.suicide_Nov.shtml#5> Accessed 28 Dec. 2006.

————. "Suicide Bill in House, Senate Shoved Aside by Impeachment Hearings." *Catholic Sentinel* 16 Oct. 1998: 1.

————. "Suicide Law Remains in Effect as Federal Judge Takes More Time to Decide." *Catholic Sentinel* 30 Nov. 2001: 1Lavery, James, and Peter Singer. "The Supremes Decide on Assisted Suicide: What Should A Doctor Do?" *Canadian Medical Journal* 157.4 (15 Aug. 1997): 405.

Lee, Barbara Coombs. Ed. *Compassion in Dying.* Troutdale: NewSage Publishing, 2003.

————. Compassion in Dying Federation Newsletter. Nov. 2001.

————. Executive Director Compassion & Choices. Personal interview. 10 Dec. 2001.

————. Compassion in Dying Federation. E-mail to author. 27 May 2004.

Lee v. Oregon, United States District Court for the District of Oregon, 891 F. Supp. 1429, 1995 US Dist.: 12011.

Lee v. Oregon, Ninth Circuit Court of Appeals, 107 F. 3d 1382 (1997).

Lee v. Oregon, Brief of intervenors-appellants/cross-appellees, Goodwin, Coombs Lee, and Sinnard. Eli Stutsman, Attorney for the Appellants, 24 Nov. 1995.

Levada, William. "Oregon's Vote in Favor of Measure 16: Report to US Bishops." April 1994, Archdiocese of San Francisco. <http://wwwsfarcdiiocese.org> Accessed 11 June 2007.

Levine, Brittany. "Assisted-Suicide Study Finds No Bias Against the Vulnerable; Concerns Focus on Elderly, Poor, Minorities." *USA Today.* 17 Oct, 2007: 9D.

"Liberty on the March." Compassion & Choices 2011 Annual Report, 2011.

LifeSite Daily News 3 July 2002, Washington D.C. <www/lifesite.net/ldn/2002/Jul/020703html> Accessed 22 Dec. 2006.

Liptak, Adam. "Ruling Upholds Oregon Law Authorizing Assisted Suicide." *The New York Times* 27 May 2004: A1.

Lodzinski, Dave. State of Oregon, Voters' Pamphlet compiled and distributed by Phil Keisling, Secretary of State, Special Election, 4 Nov. 1997.

Long, James. "Churches Denounce Suicide Bill." *Oregonian* 19 Sept. 1994: B1.

Lowe, Dylan Alexandra. "Facing the Final Exit." *ABA Journal* 83 A.B.A.J. 48 (Sep. 1997): 3. Accessed 8 Mar. 2008.

Lucas, Maya. "Justices Asked to End Oregon's Act." *Legal Times* 16 Feb. 2005 <law.com> Accessed 20 Feb. 2005.

Lunch, Bill. Comments of a political science professor and political analyst on "Seven Days." Oregon Public Broadcasting, 7 Nov. 1997.

———. "The Politics of Death: Assisted Suicide Policy and Politics, in Oregon and the Nation." A paper presented to the 1998 Annual Meeting of the Western Political Science Association, Los Angeles, CA, 20 Mar. 1998.

Lunge, Robin, Maria Royle, and Michael Slater. "Oregon's Death with Dignity Law and Euthanasia in the Netherlands: Factual Disputes." Legislative Council, State of Vermont, 2004.

Lynch, Gregory P. Brief for Amicus Physicians for Compassionate Care Education Foundation in Support of Petitioners for the Supreme Court of the United States in the case of *Gonzales v. Oregon:* Appendix A.

Mahood, H. R. *Interest Groups in American National Politics.* Upper Saddle River: Prentice Hall, 2000.

Mann, Damian. "Locally Issue Gets Mixed Reviews." *Mail Tribune* 18 Feb. 2006: 1A.

Mapes, Jeff. "Lieberman Favors Banning Assisted Suicide." *Oregonian* 12 Oct. 2000: A5.

———. "Strong Support for Assisted-Suicide Measure." *Oregonian* 27 Oct 1994: 2.

Marker, Rita. "Assisted Suicide and Death with Dignity: Past, Present, and Future." International Task Force on Euthanasia and Assisted Suicide Website. 2008. <http//www.internationaltaksforce.org/rpy2005/htm> Accessed 26 Nov. 2008.

———. Euthanasia and Assisted Suicide Task Force Website. "Assisted Suicide: The Continuing Debate." n.d. <http//wwwinternationaltaskforce.org/cd.htm.> Accessed 28 Nov. 2008.

McAtee, Shendy. "Assisted-Suicide Better than Violent Alternative." Letter. *Oregonian* 29 Oct. 1997, B15.

McCord, Hugo. "Death With Dignity"?. Christian Articles, <www.christianarticles.org> Accessed 12 March 2012.

"Measure 16: What It Says." *Oregonian* 30 Oct. 1994: D05.

Melchoir, Jill A. "Casenote: The Quiet Battle for the Heart of Liberty—A Victory for the Cautious: *Washington v. Glucksberg.*" 117 S. Ct. 2258, 1997, *University of Cincinnati Law Review,* Summer 1998, 66 U. Cin. Rev. 1359: 1-212.

Meir, David, Carol-Ann Emmons, Sylvan Wallenstein, Timothy Quill, Sean Morrison, and Christine Cassel. "A National Survey of Physician-Assisted Suicide and Euthanasia in the United States." *New England Journal of Medicine* 338.17 (1998): 1193–1201.

Montana Constitution Art II, Sec 4 and 10, 6 June 1972.

"Montana Judge: Man Has Right To Assisted Suicide." *Mail Tribune* 7 Dec. 2008: 6A.

Moore, Mark H. *Creating Public Value.* Cambridge: Harvard University Press, 1995.

Nelson, Barbara J. *Making An Issue of Child Abuse.* Chicago: University of Chicago Press, 1984.

"News, Assisted Suicide Chronology." *Oregonian* 2 Dec. 2000: A1.

"The Next Steps to the Next State." *The Dignity Report:* (Spring 2009) 1.

No On I-1000 Website. <http//www.noassistedsuicide.com.> Accessed 28 Nov. 2008.

Official Abstract of Votes, County of Lincoln, State of Oregon. 4 Nov. 1997, Special election dtd. 12 Nov. 1997.

Official 1994 General Election Voters' Pamphlet, Elections Department, State of Oregon, Statewide.

Official 1997 General Election Voters' Pamphlet, Elections Department, State of Oregon, Measure 51: 1.

O'Keefe, Mark. "Analyzing the Ads." *Oregonian* 11 Oct. 1994: B4.

———. "Assisted-Suicide Measure Survives Heavy Opposition." *Oregonian* 10 Nov. 1994: A1.

———. "Expensive Acrimonious Campaigns Expected for November Election." *Oregonian* 27 June 1997: A22.

———. "Founding Father." *Oregonian* 1 Nov. 1994: A12.

———. "Freedom from Religion." *Oregonian* 9 Nov. 1997: G1.

———. "Hemlock Society Director Praises Oregon's Lead Role." *Oregonian* 28 June 1998: D13.

———. "House Approves Asking for Repeal of Suicide Law." *Oregonian* 14 May 1997: A1.

———. "Oregon Agonizes on Moral Issues." *Oregonian* 9 Nov. 1994: B5.

———. "Testimony Clashes on Suicide Measure." *Oregonian* 13 Mar. 1997: E3.

———. "TV Ad on Assisted Suicide Leaves Out Part of Story." *Oregonian* 4 Nov. 1994: C1.

O'Keefe, Mark, and Tom Bates. "Freedom To Die." *Oregonian* 5 Jan. 1997: B1.

O'Keefe, Mark, and Ashbel Green. "Court Lifts Injunction." *Oregonian* 5 Nov. 1997: A1.

O'Keefe, Mark, and Patrick O'Neill. "Court Confirms Right to Die." *Oregonian* 7 Mar. 1996: A1.

Okie, Susan. "I Should Die the Way I Want To." *Washington Post* 1 Jan. 2002: A1.

Omandam, Pat. "Legislature Will Consider Euthanasia." *Honolulu Star-Bulletin* 10 June 1998. <http://starbulletin.com/98/06/10/news/story3.html> Accessed 28 Dec. 2006.

"One Year Later: Lessons from Terri Schiavo." Compassion & Dying Top Stories, 30 Aug 2006. <http://compassionandchoices.org> Accessed 7 May 2007.

O'Neill, Patrick. *Eighth Annual Report on Oregon's Death with Dignity Act*. 10 <http://egov.Oregon.gov/DHS?ph/pas/> Accessed 22 April 2006.

———. "Suicide Debate Vital to Democracy." *Oregonian* 8 Dec. 1997: A1.

"Oregon's Assisted Suicide Experience." Omega Publications, Salem, OR. n.d.

"Oregon's Assisted Suicide Law." *Religion and Ethics* 31 Oct. 1997: 1.

Oregon Death with Dignity Act. Oregon Revised Statutes, 127; 880, 3.13.

Oregon Death with Dignity. Report on improvements in end-of-life care 2002 by Oregon Death with Dignity Legal Defense and Education Center, Portland OR.

Oregon Department of Health Services News Release. 9 Mar. 2004.

Oregon Elections Division, Oregon Measure 16. (Election date 4 Nov. 1994). 12 June 2007.

———. Oregon Catholic Conference Web page .<www.archpdx/prig/PCC/> 22 Dec. 2006. Accessed 17 June 2007.

The Oregon Death with Dignity Act, Oregon Revised Statutes. 127; 880, 3.13.

"Oregon Law Should Stand." Editorial. *St. Petersburg Times* 24 Feb. 2005. <www.sptimes.comm/2005/02/24/Opinion/Oregon_Law> 2006. Accessed 28 Dec. 2006.

Oregon Legislative Minutes. 1997 regular session, Minutes of the House Committee on Judiciary, Subcommittee on Family Law.

———. 12 Mar. 1997, Tape 38A, 338.

———. 12 Mar. 1997, Tape 42A, 232.

———. 12 Mar, 1997, Tape 44A, 126.

———. 12 Mar. 1997, Tape 44A, 150.

———. 12 Mar. 1997. Tape 45A, 353.

———. 13 Mar. 1997, Tape 47B, 386.

Oregon Right to Life Press Release on Ashcroft Ruling. 6 Nov. 2001. <www.ortl.org> Accessed 14 Mar. 2012.

Oregon v. Ashcroft. US Court of Appeals for the Ninth Circuit. 04-623. Nov. 9, 2004. On Petition for a Writ of Certiorari 2004 WL 2544622 (U.S.): 1.

Oregon v. Ashcroft. US Court of Appeals for the Ninth Circuit. CV-01-01647-JO. Opinion Argued and Submitted 7 May 2003 and filed 26 May 2004. 02-35587 D.C. I: 6616.

Oregon v. Ashcroft. Permanent Injunction in US District Court for the District of Oregon. CV 01-1647-JO. 17 April 2002.

Oregon v. Ashcroft. US District Court for the District of Oregon. CV 01-1647, Transcript of Temporary Restraining Order: 9, lines 13-20. 9 Nov. 2001.

Ostrom, Carol. "At Least 36 Die Using Washington State's New Law." *Mail Tribune* 5 March 2010: 2A.

Packard, Melissa. Maine Director of Elections and Commissions, E-mail to author. 9 August 2007.

Patient Choice and Control at End of Life Act in 2007 (H 44). Bill as introduced 2007. VT LEG 211335, 2.

Permanent Injunction in the case of *Oregon v. Ashcroft* in the US District Court for the District of Oregon. Civil 01-1647-JO. Judge Jones presiding. 17 April 2002.

Pearsall, John. "Reader Feedback." *Oregonian* 22 Oct. 1997: C13.

Petty, Bill, Board of Directors. Physicians for Compassionate Care. Personal interview. 8 Nov. 2000.

Pfleger, Katherine. "Wyden Urges Bush to Lay Off Assisted Suicide Law." *Mail Tribune* 31 Oct. 2001: 5A.

Physicians for Compassionate Care, George Lynch counsel, Brief for Amicus, *Gonzales v. Oregon* 64-623 in the Supreme Court of the United States in support of petitioners, 9 May 2005.

Physicians for Compassionate Care Educational Foundation Website. <www.pccef.org> 21 April 2007. Accessed 22 Nov. 2008.

————. "Assisted-Suicide Experiment Has Failed." 19 Feb. 2001:1.

————. "Assisted Suicide Report Plagued by Shortcomings." 23 Feb. 2000: 1.

————. Education Committee. Press Release, 9 Mar. 2006: 1.

————. News, 3.3 Fall 2000.

————. Newsletter. 4.1 (Spring 2001): 4.

————. Press Release. 30 June 2006: 1.

————. Press Release. 27 Jan. 2011.

————. Press Release. 8 Mar. 2012.

"Progress is Underway for Terminally Ill Patients in Washington and New York States." *The Body, The Complete HIV/AIDS Resource*. Compassion in Dying, Issue 3, 27 (December 2006): I.

Rawls, John, et al., "Assisted Suicide: The Philosophers Brief." *New York Times Review of Books* 26 Mar. 1997: 27.

Reinhard, David. "In the Dark Shadows of Measure 16." *Oregonian* 31 Oct. 1999: D5.

———. "Is Uncle Sam Beating Up on Poor Oregon?" *Oregonian* 24 Feb. 2005: D7.

———. "Liar, Liar." *Oregonian* 19 Oct. 1997: E4.

———. "Measure 16: The Vote of Your Life." *Oregonian* 27 Oct. 1994: D10.

Reporting forms and the physician's questionnaire <http://www.dhs.state.or.us/publichealth/chs/pas/pasforms.ctm> Accessed 27 Dec. 2006.

Ricci, James. "Right-to-die Bill Failure Again Linked to Mistrust." *Mail Tribune* 8 Aug. 2007: I.

"The Rights of the Terminally Ill." Editorial. *New York Times* 28 May 2004: A22.

Roberts, Barbara. "Get the Facts Straight." YouTube 29 Oct. 2008.

Roosevelt, Margot. "Choosing Their Time." *Time* 4 April 2005: 31.

Rosenblatt, Susan. "Activists Rally to Redlands Doctor's Cause." *Los Angeles Times* 12 Sep. 2006. <http://www.dwd.org/news/news/latimes> Accessed 30 July 2007.

Rubenstein, Sura. "Storm Brews Over Right to Die." *Oregonian* 6 Dec. 1993: BI.

Sahr, Robert, and Susan Banducci. "The Oregon 1994 General Election Exit Poll." Oregon State University Political Science Department, 1994.

Sandeen, Peg. Death with Dignity National Center. Personal interview. 15 Aug. and 17 Sep. 2007.

Sanford, Janice. "Justice for Terri Schiavo." 29 May 2007, a blog at <justice1949@aol.com> Accessed 19 July 2007.

Schwartz, John, and James Estrin. "Conversations About Death." *Oregonian* 31 Mar. 2005: A8.

———. "In Oregon, Choosing Death Over Suffering." *New York Times* I June 2004: D4.

———. "In Vermont, a Bid to Legalize Physician-Assisted Suicide." *New York Times* 20 Mar. 2005 <http://newyorktimes.com.> Accessed 28 Dec. 2006.

"Senate Sends Suicide Law Back to Voters." *Mail Tribune* 6 June 1997. <http//www/mailtribune/archive/97/june/61097n3.htm.> Accessed 15 Nov. 2007.

Shapiro. David. "Enact Death with Dignity." *Honolulu Advertiser* 5 Feb. 2003: I.

Sheen, Martin. "Yes on I-1000" (I-1000). YouTube. 31 Oct. 2008. <http://www.youtube.com/watch?v=T-DwFmZpol/w> Accessed 11 Dec. 2008.

Sheley, Kim. E-mail to author. 8 Oct. 2008.

Smigelski, David. "To Lie For." *Willamette Week* 17 Sep. 1997: I.

————. "The Moral Minority." *Willamette Week* 14 May 1997. <http:/www.positiveartheism.org/writ/wwmm.htm> Accessed 27 Dec. 2006.

Smith, Wesley J. "Suing For the Right to Assisted Suicide." 18 Oct. 2007 <www.weslyjsmith.com> Accessed 8 Dec. 2008.

Sneyd, Ross. "House Votes Down Assisted Suicide Bill." *Associated Press* 21 Mar. 2007 <http://web.lexix-nexis.com.proxy.tui.edu/universe> Accessed 20 July 2007.

————. "Legislature Opens Debate on Death with Dignity." *Associated Press* 23 Feb. 2007 <http://web.lexix-nexis.com.proxy.tui.edu/universe> Accessed 20 July 2007.

Song, Jaymes. "Report Gives Hawaii Mixed Grades for End of Life Care." *Associated Press.* <http://web.lexis-nexis.com/universe/document?m=7f790bb006c67bdfed5eb3cd0034> Accessed 28 Dec. 2006.

Sorokin, Michael. Lobbyist Vermont Death with Dignity. Personal interview. 16 July 2008.

State of Oregon General Election Voters' Pamphlet. Elections Department, State of Oregon, Statewide Measures 4 Nov. 1994.

Stevens, Kenneth. "Debating Assisted Suicide." Christian Life Resources, Milwaukee, WI. Videotape of presentation at Clearly Caring Convention, 13 October 2004.

————. President. Physicians for Compassionate Care. Personal interview. 14 Aug. 2007.

Stevens, Kenneth, and William Toffler. "Assisted Suicide: Conspiracy and Control." *Oregonian* 24 Sep. 2008. <http://blog.oregonlive.com/opinion_impacct> Accessed 15 June 2009.

Stone, Deborah. *Policy Paradox.* New York: W.W. Norton Company, 1988.

Stutsman, Eli D. Legal Counsel National Death with Dignity. Personal interview, 4, 8, and 27 June 2007.

————. "Political Strategy and Legal Change," Quill, Timothy, and Margaret Battin, Eds. *Physician-Assisted Dying.* Baltimore: John Hopkins Press, 2004, 252.

2008 Summary of Oregon's Death with Dignity Act. <www.oregon.gov/dhs/ph/pas> Accessed 15 June 2009.

2011 Summary of Oregon's Death with Dignity Act. <www.oregon.gov/dhs/ph/pas> Accessed 10 Mar. 2012.

2011 Summary of Oregon's Death With Dignity Act. Table I <www.oregon.gov/dhs/ph/pas> Accessed 10 Mar. 2012.

"Suicide Law Defies Prediction." *Mail Tribune* 9 Mar. 2001: IA.

Suo, Steve. "Big Purse Expected for Round Two." *Oregonian* 10 June 1997: AI.

Suo, Steve, and Jeff Mapes. "Measure 8 Sponsors Won't List Donors." *Oregonian* 9 Dec. 1994: D9.

"The Supreme Court Considers Challenge to Oregon's Death with Dignity Act." Pew Forum on Religion and Public Life. 30 Sep. 2005: 11.

"Supreme Court's Decision in *Gonzales v. Oregon.*" The Pew Research Center, Legal Backgrounder, Jan. 2006: 3.

Thompson, Sandy, Candidate Registrar, Maine Commission on Governmental Ethics and Election Practices. E-mail to author. 19 Oct. 2007.

Tibbits. George. "Eleven End Lives Using Washington State Suicide Law So Far." *Mail Tribune* 9 Sep. 2009: 7A.

Toffler, William. National Director, Physicians for Compassionate Care. Personal interview. 14 Aug. 2007.

————. "Ratification of Assisted-Suicide by Oregon: Lessons Learned." Handout, Sep. 1998.

Tolle, Susan, Virginia P. Tilden, Linda L. Drach, Erik K. Fromme, Nancy A. Perrin, and Katrina Hedberg. "Characteristics and Proportion of Dying Oregonians Who Personally Consider Physician-Assisted Suicide." *The Journal of Clinical Ethics* 15.2 (2004): 112.

Tu, Janet. "New Ads, Barbs Over I-1000." *The Seattle Times* 31 Oct. 2008.

Tucker, Kathryn L. "Privacy and Dignity at the End of Life: Protecting the Right Of Montanans to Choose Aid in Dying." *Montana Law Review* 68.2

(Summer 2007): 318. <http:seattletimes.nesource.com> Accessed 26 Nov. 2008.

Turner, Joseph. "Catholic Parishes Raising Money." *The News Tribune* 2 Sep. 2008.

———. "Voters Will Decide In November, Catholics Start Fight Against Initiative." *The News Tribune* 3 Sept. 2008: B01.

Turner, Joseph, and Anna Walters. "Catholic Church Solicits Money to Defeat Assisted Suicide Initiative." *Bellingham Herald* 4 Sep. 2008 <http://www.bellinghamherald.com> Accessed 26 Nov. 2008.

Uherbelau, Judy. Representative Oregon House. Personal interview. 2 Nov. 2002.

US House of Representatives Committee on the Judiciary. Henry J. Hyde, Chairman <www.house.gov/judiciary/ib0622399htm> Accessed 28 Dec. 2006.

"US Supreme Court Rules Federal Government Does Not Have Authority to Block Oregon Physician Assisted Suicide Law." *Medical News Today* 19 Jan. 2006 <http://www.medicalnewstoday.com/medicalnews.php?newsid=36285&aridsr5sfseds> Accessed 28 Dec. 2006.

Verhovek, Sam Howe. "Oregon Chafes at Measure to Stop Assisted Suicides." *New York Times* 29 Oct. 1999: A1.

———. "US Acts to Stop Physicians Who Assist Suicides in Oregon." *New York Times* 7 Nov. 2001: A1.

Vermont Compassion & Choices Website. <http:www//choicesvermont.org> Accessed 28 Dec. 2006.

Vermont General Assembly, Act. 166, Palliative Care; End-of-Life Care; Pain Management, effective date: 1 July 2008.

Vermont General Assembly, Hearings on Senate Bill 281, 21 January 2008, attended by author.

"Victory in the Vermont State House." Vermont Right to Life Committee, 22 Mar. 2007. <www.vrlcnet/VRLCMaihfiles/VictoryOverPAShtml> Accessed 20 July 2007.

Walker, Jack. "The Diffusion of Innovations Among the States." *American Political Science Review* 63 (Sep. 1969): 895.

Walters, Dick. President Vermont Death with Dignity. Personal interview. 18 July 2007.

Washington v. Glucksberg. 117 S. Ct. 2258, 138 L.Ed. 2d. 772 (1997). 17. Supreme Court Collection. 26 June 1997. 11 pgs. 6 May 2001. <http//www-4law.cornell.edu.> Accessed 27 Dec. 2006.

Washington v. Glucksberg, Oral Argument, Transcript in the Supreme Court of the United States, 96–110, 8 Jan. 1997.

Washington Secretary of State, Elections, 4 Nov. 2008, General Election. <http//vote.wa.gov/elections/wei/results> Accessed 26 Nov. 2008.

Washington State Public Disclosure Commission, database of contributions, n.d. <www.pdc.wa.gov/servlet/InitContServlet> Accessed 26 Nov. 2008.

Wittman, Bradley S. Director, Election Liaison Division. Michigan Department of State. Bureau of Elections, E-mail to author. 7 Aug. 2007.

Woodward, Curt. "Former WA Gov Files Assisted Suicide Initiative." *Associated Press.* 10 Jan. 2008. <http://www.lexisnexis.com> Accessed 1 Dec. 2008.

Wyden, Ron. "Pain Relief Act Will Cause More Suffering, Not Less." *Oregonian* 16 Sep. 2000. <www.oregonlive.com> Accessed 28 Dec, 2006.

———. US Senator, OR. Personal interview, 20 Aug. 2010.

———. "Statement Upon Defeat of Nickles Legislation to Overturn Oregon's Physician-Assisted Suicide Law." 15 Dec. 2000.

———. Testimony of US Senator Ron Wyden Before the Senate Committee on the Judiciary Regarding the Pain Relief Promotion Act, 25 April 2000.

Yang, Gordon. "Death with Dignity Bill Shelved." *Honolulu Advertiser* 10 Mar. 2004. <http://the.honoluluadvertiser.com/article/2004/Mar/10/In/N08a.html> Accessed 28 Dec. 2006.

Yoshimitsu, Walter. Manager Diocesan Services. Personal interview. 16 June 2003.

Young, Amalie. "Scalia Sides with Oregon's Assisted Suicide Law." *Mail Tribune* 11 Feb. 2001: 4A.

Young, Michael, Ira S. Halper, David C. Clark, William Scheftner, and Jan Fawcett. " An Item-Response Theory Evaluation of the Beck Hopelessness Scale." *Cognitive Therapy and Research* 16. 5. (Oct. 1992): 579–587.

Zalman, Marvin, John Strate, Denis Hunter, and James Sellars, "Michigan's Assisted Suicide Three Ring Circus—An Intersection of Law and Politics." *Northern University Law Review* 23.3 (1997) 863–968.

Ziegler, Stephen, and Robert Jackson. "Who's Not Afraid of Proposal B?" *Politics and Life Sciences* 23.1. (June 2006): 42–48.

Notes

Preface

1   Robert Fitzhenry, *The Harper Book of Quotations* (New York: HarperPerenial, 1993), 24.

2   Barbara J. Nelson, *Making An Issue of Child Abuse* (Chicago: University of Chicago Press, 1984), 23.

3   Barbara Coombs Lee, President, Compassion & Choices, personal interview, 10 Dec. 2001.

Chapter I

4   Tom Bates, "Elven O. Sinnard," *Oregonian* 2 Feb. 1997: B1.

5   Qtd. in Tom Bates, "Write to Die," *Oregonian* 18 Dec. 1994: A1.

6   "Elven 'Al' Sinnard Dies," *Compassion in Dying* Newsletter 8.1 (Spring 2000): 3.

7   Bates, "Write to Die" A1.

8   Bates, "Write to Die" A1.

9   Qtd. in Daniel Hillyard and John Dombrink, *Dying Right: The Death With Dignity Movement* (New York: Routledge, 2001), 79.

10   Eli D. Stutsman, Legal Counsel National Death with Dignity, personal interview, 8 June 2007.

11   Qtd in Bates, "Write to Die," A1.

12   Eli Stutsman, "Political Strategy and Legal Change." Quill, Timothy, and Margaret Battin, eds. *Physician-Assisted Dying* (Baltimore: John Hopkins Press, 2004), 252.

13   Janet Flowers, Oregon State Elections Division, e-mail to author 18 June 2007.

14   Stutsman, personal interview. 8 June 2007.

15   Sura Rubenstein, "Storm Brews Over Right To Die," *Oregonian* 6 Dec. 1993: B1.

16   Qtd. by Rubenstein B1.

17   "Measure 16: What It Says," *Oregonian* 30 Oct. 1994: D5.

18   Stutsman, personal interview, 27 June 2007.

19   Peter Goodwin, Board of Directors Oregon Compassion and Choice, personal interview, 18 June 2007.

20   Dave Hogan and Jeff Mapes, "Is Oregon Losing Its Initiative?" *Oregonian* 22 May 2003: A1.

21   Steve Suo and Jeff Mapes, "Measure 8 Sponsors Won't List Donors," *Oregonian* 9 Dec. 1994: D9.

22   William Levada, "Oregon's Vote in Favor of Measure 16: Report to US Bishops," April 1994, Archdiocese of San Francisco <http://wwwsfarcdiiocese.org> Accessed 11 June 2007.

23   Courtney S. Campbell, "The Oregon Trail to Death: Measure 16—Euthanasia Initiative," *Commonweal* 19 August 1994 <http://findarticles.com> Accessed 18 May 2007.

24   Janet Flowers, Oregon State Elections Division, e-mail to author 12 June 2007.

25   Mark O'Keefe, "Founding Father," *Oregonian* 1 Nov. 1994: A12.

26   Gail Kinsey Hill and Ashbel Green, "Initiative Campaigns Wallow in Cash," *Oregonian* 3 Nov. 1994: C7.

27   Qtd. by David Briggs, "Bishops Attack Assisted Suicide," *Oregonian* 18 Nov. 1994: A23.

28   Qtd. by James Long, "Churches Denounce Suicide Bill," *Oregonian* 19 Sep. 1994: B1.

29   David Reinhard, "Measure 16: The Vote of Your Life," *Oregonian* 27 Oct. 1994: D10.

30   Qtd. by Long B1.

31   "Campaign Watch: Measure 16: Backers Report," *Oregonian* 22 Sept. 1994: C4.

32   Qtd. by Long B1.

33   Stutsman, personal interview, 27 June 2007.

34   Mark O'Keefe, "Analyzing the Ads," *Oregonian* 11 Oct. 1994: B4.

35   Jim Davis, State of Oregon, "Voters' Pamphlet, Statewide Measures" 4 Nov. 1994: 125.

36   Mark O'Keefe, "TV Ad on Assisted Suicide Leaves Out Part of Story," *Oregonian* 4 Nov. 1994: C1.

37   Hillyard and Dombrink 89.

38   Voters' Pamphlet 125.

39   Derek Humphry, Letter, *New York Times* 3 Dec. 1994: 22.

40   O'Keefe, "Founding Father" A12.

41   Barbara Coombs Lee, President Compassion & Choices, personal interview, 10 Dec. 2001.

42   Stutsman, personal interview. 4 June 2007.

43   O'Keefe, "Founding Father" A12.

44   Phil Keisling, *Oregon Blue Book 1997-8* (Portland: Daily Journal of Commerce, 1997) 369.

45   Qtd. by O'Keefe, "Oregon Agonizes" B5.

46   Tom Bates and Mark O'Keefe, "Oregon Is a Maverick Once Again," *Oregonian* 13 Nov. 1994: A1.

47   Robert Sahr and Susan Banducci, "The Oregon 1994 General Election Exit Poll," Oregon State University Political Science Department, 1994.

48   Gail Kinsey Hill, "Kitzhaber Supports Assisted Suicide," *Oregonian* 3 Aug. 1997: A1.

49   Qtd. by Bates and O'Keefe A1.

50   Mark O'Keefe, "Assisted-Suicide Measure Survives," A1.

51   Qtd. by Tom Bates, "Vatican Article Denounces State's Assisted Suicide," *Oregonian* 1 Dec. 1994: A23.

52   Mark Duntley, "Moral Authority and Assisted Suicide," *Sojourners: Christians for Justice and Peace* May–June 1995.

53   William Toffler, "Ratification of Assisted-Suicide by Oregon: Lessons Learned," handout, Sep. 1998.

54   Qtd. by "Oregon's Assisted Suicide Law," *Religion and Ethics* 31 Oct. 1997: 1.

Chapter 2

55   Mark O'Keefe and Tom Bates, "Freedom To Die," *Oregonian* 5 Jan. 1997: B1.

56   Oregon Legislative Minutes, 1997 regular session, Minutes of the House Committee on Judiciary, Subcommittee on Family Law, 12 Mar. 1997, Tape 42A, 232.

57 Qtd. by Mark O'Keefe, "Testimony Clashes on Suicide Measure," *Oregonian* 13 Mar. 1997: E3.

58 Qtd. by Mark O'Keefe, "Testimony Clashes," E3.

59 Kenneth Stevens, President Physicians for Compassionate Care, personal interview, 14 August 2007.

60 "Beyond Red and Blue," Pew Research Center, <http:www.people-press. org> Accessed 27 Dec. 2006.

61 Gail Kinsey Hill, "Kitzhaber Supports Assisted Suicide," *Oregonian* 3 Aug. 1997"A1.

62 George, Eighmey, Executive Director Oregon Compassion and Dying, personal interview, 13 August 2007.

63 Ed Langlois, "Legislators Bring Suicide Flaws to the Surface," *Catholic Sentinel* 21 Mar. 1997: 1.

64 Oregon Legislative Minutes, 1997 regular session, Minutes of the House Committee on Judiciary, Subcommittee on Family Law, 11 Mar. 1997, Tape 47B, 386.

65 Qtd. by O'Keefe, "Testimony" E3.

66 O'Keefe, "Testimony" E3.

67 Oregon Legislative Minutes, Tape 44A, 126.

68 Oregon Legislative Minutes, Tape 44A, 150.

69 Oregon Legislative Minutes, Tape 47B, 386.

70 O'Keefe, "Testimony" E3.

71 Oregon Legislative Minutes, Tape 38 A, 338.

72 Langlois 1.

73 Oregon Legislative Minutes, Tape 45A, 353.

74 Qtd. by Mark O'Keefe, "House Approves Asking for Repeal of Suicide Law," *Oregonian* 14 May, 1997: A1.

75 Eighmey, personal interview.

76 David Smigelski, "The Moral Minority," *Willamette Weekly* 14 May 1997 <http:/www.positiveatheism.org/writ/wwmm.htm> Accessed 27 December 2006.

77 Qtd. in Editorial, "Death Without Dignity," *Oregonian* 11 May 1997: E4.

78 Qtd. by Mark O'Keefe, "House Approves" A1.

79 Qtd. by O'Keefe, "House Approves" A1.

80 Ed Langlois 1.

81   O'Keefe, "House Approves" AI.

82   Qtd. by O'Keefe, "House Approves" AI.

83   Qtd. by O'Keefe, "House Approves" AI.

84   Ashbel S. Green, "Suicide Law Returns to Voters," *Oregonian* 10 June 1997: AI.

85   Qtd. by Green AI.

86   Qtd. by Green AI.

87   "Senate Sends Suicide Law Back to Voters," *Mail Tribune* 6 June 1997: AI.

88   Adapted from Dr. Bill Lunch, "The Politics of Death: Assisted Suicide Policy and Politics, in Oregon and the Nation," 20 Mar. 1998, a paper presented to the 1998 Annual Meeting of the Western Political Science Association, Los Angeles, CA: 14.

89   Lunch 14.

90   Judy Uherbelau, personal interview, 2 Nov. 2002.

91   O'Keefe, "House Approves" AI.

92   Qtd. by Smigelski.

93   Steve Suo, "Big Purse Expected for Round Two," *Oregonian* 10 June 1997: AI.

94   Mark O'Keefe, "Expensive Acrimonious Campaigns Expected for November Election," *Oregonian*, 27 June 1997: A22.

95   E. J. Dionne, "Lively Debate on Dying," *Oregonian* 30 June 1997: B12.

96   Qtd. by Daniel Hillyard and John Dombrink, *Dying Right: The Death With Dignity Movement* (New York: Routledge, 2001), 103.

97   Langlois I.

Chapter 3

98   Bill Petty, Board of Directors, Physicians for Compassionate Care, personal interview, 8 Nov. 2000.

99   Amy Corneliussen, "Controversial Judge Dismisses Detractors," *Corvallis Gazette-Times* 19 Jan. 1998: I.

100 Barbara Coombs Lee, ed., *Compassion in Dying* (Troutdale: NewSage Publishing, 2003) 133.

101 Qtd. by Dee Lane, "Judges Decision on Measure 16 Stirs Conflicting Views," *Oregonian* 29 Dec. 1994: A7.

102 Spencer Heinz and Mark O'Keefe, "Judge Puts Suicide Law on Hold," *Oregonian* 28 Dec. 1994: A1.

103 Editorial, "Protect the Dying," *Oregonian* 5 Aug. 1995: D4.

104 *Lee v. Oregon*, United States District Court for the District of Oregon 891 F. Supp. 1429; 1995 US Dist. Lexis 12011.

105 Thomas A. Balmer, personal interview, 25 June 2007.

106 *Lee v. Oregon*, Brief of intervenors-appellants/cross-appellees, Goodwin, Coombs Lee, and Sinnard. Eli Stutsman, Attorney for the Appellants, 24 Nov. 1995: 23.

107 Spencer Heinz, "Assisted Suicide: Advocates Weigh In," *Oregonian* 9 Dec. 1994: A1.

108 David J. Garrow, "Nine Justices and a Funeral," *George* June 1997: 56.

109 *Compassion in Dying v. Washington*, 1996, Ninth Circuit Court of Appeals (en banc), 850F Supp at 1455-57.

110 Daniel Hillyard and John Dombrink, *Dying Right: The Death With Dignity Movement* (New York: Routledge, 2001) 125.

111 *Compassion in Dying v. Washington*, 1994, United States District Court for the Western District of Washington, Seattle Division, 850 F. Supp. 1454; 1994 US Dist.

112 "Progress Is Underway for Terminally Ill Patients in Washington and New York States," *The Body, The Complete HIV/AIDS Resource*, Compassion in Dying, Issue 3, 27 (December 2006): 1.

113 *Compassion in Dying v. Washington*, 1996, Ninth US Circuit Court of Appeals, 79 F, 3d 790:1196 US App.

114 Qtd. in "Court Hears Case for Assisted Suicide," *Oregonian* 27 Oct. 1995: C11.

115 "Court Hears Case" C11.

116 Alexandra Dylan Lowe, "Facing the Final Exit," *ABA Journal* 83 A.B.A.J. 48 (Sep. 1997): 3.

117 Qtd. by *Compassion in Dying v. State of Washington* 1996: 1455-57.

118 Mark O'Keefe and Patrick O'Neill, "Court Confirms Right to Die," *Oregonian* 7 Mar. 1996: A1.

119 "Court Confuses Liberty, Death," editorial, *Oregonian* 4 Mar. 1996: C8.

120 Derek Humphry, "Perspectives on Assisted Suicide," *Los Angeles Times* 8 Mar. 1996: B11.

121 Qtd. by Tom Bates, "Suicide Injunction Stands," *Oregonian* 24 April 1996: CI.

122 Qtd by Bates CI.

123 Brief Amicus Curiae of the American Hospital Association, *Glucksberg v. Washington* <http://uphs.upenn.edu/-bioethic/PAS/Sa.html> Accessed 27 Dec. 2006.

124 Joseph Howard, "American Bioethics Advisory Committee," <http://all.org/abac/ch001.htm> Accessed 27 Dec. 2006.

125 H. R. Mahood, *Interest Groups in American National Politics* (Upper Saddle River: Prentice Hall, 2000), 131–32, Table 8.2 Analysis of Amicus Briefs in Opposition to Doctor-Assisted Suicide Right.

126 John Rawls, et al., "Assisted Suicide: The Philosophers Brief," *New York Times Review of Books* 26 Mar 1997: 27.

127 H. R. Mahood 126–27, Table 8.1 Analysis of Amicus Briefs in Support of a Doctor-Assisted Suicide Right.

128 Qtd. by Garrow 59.

129 Qtd. by Garrow 59.

130 *Washington v. Glucksberg*, Oral Argument, Transcript in the Supreme Court of the United States 96-110, 8 Jan. 1997.

131 Jill A. Melchoir, "Casenote: The Quiet Battle for the Heart of Liberty—A Victory for the Cautious: *Washington v. Glucksberg*" 117 S. Ct. 2258 (1997), *University of Cincinnati Law Review*, Summer, 1998, 66 U. Cin. Rev.1359: 1.

132 *Washington v. Glucksberg* 117 S. Ct. 2258, 138 L.Ed. 2d. 772 (1997), 17. Supreme Court Collection. 26 June 1997. 11 pgs. 6 May 2001.

133 *Washington v. Glucksberg* 17.

134 James Lavery and Peter Singer, "The Supremes Decide on Assisted Suicide: What Should A Doctor Do?" *Canadian Medical Journal* 157.4 (15 Aug. 1997): 405.

135 Melchoir 212.

136 Qtd. by Mark O'Keefe and Ashbel Green, "Court Lifts Injunction," *Oregonian* 5 Nov. 1997: A1.

137 *Lee v. Oregon*, 1997, Ninth Circuit Court of Appeals, 107 F. 3d 1382.

138 News, Assisted Suicide Chronology, *Oregonian* 2 Dec. 2000: A1.

139 O'Keefe and Green A1.

140 Reporting forms and the physician's questionnaire are available at <http://www.dhs.state,or.us/publichealth/chs/pas/pasforms.ctm> Accessed 27 Dec. 2006.

141 Qtd. by Gail Hill and Erin Hoover, "Two Die Using Suicide Law," *Oregonian* 26 Mar. 1998: A1.

142 N. Greg Hamilton, "Assisted Suicide Puts Patients at Risk," *Washington Times* 29 Sept. 2000.

143 Qtd. by Gail Kinsey Hill, "Legislators Discuss Special Session," *Oregonian* 6 Nov. 1997: A1.

144 Hillyard and Dombrink 201.

145 George Eighmey, Executive Director Oregon Compassion and Dying, personal interview, 13 August 2007.

146 John Dinan, "Rights and the Political Process: Physician-Assisted Suicide in the Aftermath of *Washington v. Glucksberg,*" *Publius: The Journal of Federalism* (2001, 31.4), 4.

147 "Court Confuses Liberty, Death" C8.

148 Erin Hoover Barnett and Ashbel S. Green, "Assisted-suicide Law Faces New Challenges in Court, Congress," *Oregonian* 12 July 1998: A1.

Chapter 4

149 Qtd. by Gail Kinsey Hill, "Kitzhaber Vetoes Assisted-Suicide Ballot Title," *Oregonian* 30 July 1997: E5.

150 Official 1997 General Election Voters' Pamphlet, Elections Department, State of Oregon, Measure 51: 2.

151 Roger Gafke and David Leuthold, "The Effect on Voters of Misleading and Difficult Ballot Titles," *The Public Opinion Quarterly* 43.3 (Autumn 1979): 398.

152 Daniel Hillyard and John Dombrink, *Dying Right: The Death With Dignity Movement* (New York: Routledge, 2001) 105.

153 Qtd. by Gail Kinsey Hill and Mark O'Keefe, "Church Follows New Political Path," *Oregonian* 16 Oct. 1997: A01.

154 Steve Suo, "Big Purse Expected for Round Two," *Oregonian* 10 June 1997: A1.

155 Qtd. by Gail Kinsey Hill, "Oregon Could Set Course on Suicide Debate in U.S.," *Oregonian* 25 Sep. 1997: A1.

156 Suo AI.

157 Qtd by Mark O'Keefe, "Expensive, Acrimonious Campaigns Expected for November Election," *Oregonian* 27 June 1997: 22.

158 Hillyard and Dombrink 105.

159 Hill and O'Keefe AI.

160 Ed Langlois, "In a Steady Rise, Record Number Used Oregon's Assisted-Suicide Law in 2003," *Catholic Sentinel* I Jan. 2004: I.

161 Gail Kinsey Hill, "Message Same as Vote Nears End," *Oregonian* 3 Nov. 1997: AI.

162 Qtd. by Hill, "Message Same," AI.

163 Susan Jay, "Suicide Aid, Round 2," *Mail Tribune* 10 Oct. 1997: I.

164 Barbara Coombs Lee, President, Compassion & Choices, personal interview, 10 Dec. 2001.

165 Hill, "Ad Wars" A8.

166 Hillyard and Dombrink 114.

167 Hillyard and Dombrink 105.

168 Qtd. by "Oregon's Assisted Suicide Law," *Religion and Ethics* 31 Oct. 1997: I.

169 Qtd. in International Task Force on Euthanasia and Assisted Suicide, "Oregon Takes a Closer Look at Assisted Suicide," 11.4 (August-October 1997) I.

170 Qtd. by Hillyard and Dombrink 106.

171 David Reinhard, "Liar, Liar," *Oregonian* 19 Oct. 1997: E4.

172 David Smigelski, "To Lie For," *Willamette Week* 17 Sep. 1997: I.

173 Arden R. Benson, letter, *Oregonian* 26 Oct. 1997: E5.

174 Shendy McAtee, "Assisted-Suicide Better than Violent Alternative," letter *Oregonian* 29 Oct. 1997, B15.

175 Official 1997 General Election Voters' Pamphlet, Measure 51: 10.

176 1997 Voters' Pamphlet, I.

177 Bill Bradbury, *Oregon Blue Book 2005-2006* (Oregon Daily Journal of Commerce 1997) 299.

178 Qtd by Hillyard and Dombrink 112.

179 Barbara Coombs Lee, President, Compassion & Choices, personal interview, 10 Dec. 2001.

180 Hugo McCord, "Death With Dignity"?, Christian Articles, <www.christianarticles.org> Accessed 12 March 2012.

181 Gail Kinsey Hill, "The Ad Wars," *Oregonian* 3 Nov. 1997: A8.

182 Bill Lunch, Comments of a political science professor and political analyst on "Seven Days." Oregon Public Broadcasting, 7 Nov. 1997.

183 Official Abstract of Votes, County of Lincoln, State of Oregon, 4 Nov. 1997, Special Election dtd. 12 Nov. 1997.

184 Adam Davis and Tim Hibbitts, Oregon Statewide Poll Conducted by Market Decisions Corporation for the *Oregonian* Sep. 1997.

185 Gail Kinsey Hill, "Inside, Not Outside Influences Guide s Voters on Measure 51," *Oregonian,* 30 Oct. 1997: AI.

186 Ed Langlois, "Pro-Euthanasia Oregon Voters Driven by Anger at Legislature," *Catholic Sentinel* 19 Dec. 1997: I.

187 John Schwartz and James Estrin, "In Oregon, Choosing Death Over Suffering," *New York Times* I June 2004: D4.

188 Peter Goodwin, Board Member Oregon Compassion & Choices, personal interview, 18 June 2007.

189 Qtd. by Schwartz and Estrin D4.

190 John Pearsall, "Reader Feedback," *Oregonian* 22 Oct. 1997: C13.

191 Langlois, "Pro-Euthanasia," I.

192 Steve Duin, "Votin' Gloatin', Pioneers," *Oregonian* 9 Nov. 1997: BI.

193 Ellen Goodman, "Nation Turns to Oregon," *Oregonian* 8 Nov. 1997: D6.

194 Qtd. by Erin Hoover, "Suicide Laws Unlikely Elsewhere," *Oregonian* 18 Nov. 1997: AI.

195 Qtd. by Patrick O'Neill, "Suicide Debate Vital to Democracy," *Oregonian* 8 Dec. 1997: AI.

196 Hill, "Inside, Not Outside," AI.

197 Qtd. by O'Neil AI.

Chapter 5

198 Qtd. by Erin Hoover Barnett, "Dilemma of Assisted Suicide: When?" *Oregonian* 17 Jan. 1999: AI.

199 Erin Hoover Barnett, "Dilemma," AI.

200 N. Greg Hamilton, "Physicians for Compassionate Care on Coos Bay Death," Press Release, Physicians for Compassionate Care, 11 Mar. 1999.

201 Physicians for Compassionate Care Press Release, "Assisted Suicide Report Plagued by Shortcomings," 23 Feb. 2000: I.

202 Thomas A. Constantine, letter from DEA administrator to Representative Henry Hyde, 5 Nov. 1997.

203 Jim Barnett, "The Insider and the Gadfly," *Oregonian* 23 April 2000: DI.

204 Congressional Record, 27 Sep. 1998: S10883.

205 Ron Wyden, Testimony of US Senator Before the Senate Committee on the Judiciary Regarding the Pain Relief Promotion Act, 25 April 2000.

206 *In Brief*, Press Release, 5 June 1998, US House of Representatives Committee on the Judiciary, Henry J. Hyde, Chairman <www.house.gov/judiciary/ib0622399htm> Accessed 28 Dec. 2006.

207 Qtd. by David Brandt-Erichsen, *Congress Daily*, 25 Sep. 1998. <www.cryonet.org> Accessed 13 March 2012.

208 Qtd. by Jim Barnett and Dave Hogan, "House Panel Votes to Block Suicide Law," *Oregonian* 5 Aug. 1998: AI.

209 Qtd. by John Hughes, "House Measure Attacks Suicide Law," *Mail Tribune* 5 Aug. 1998: 5A.

210 Qtd. by Hughes 5A.

211 Ed Langlois, "Suicide Bill in House, Senate Shoved Aside by Impeachment Proceedings," *Catholic Sentinel* 16 Oct. 1998: I.

212 Congressional Record, 27 Sep. 1998: S10883.

213 Jim Barnett and Dave Hogan, "Senate Panel OKs Suicide Ban," *Oregonian* 25 Sep. 1998: AI.

214 Barnett and Hogan, "Senate Panel," AI.

215 Congressional Record, 14 Oct. 1998: S12491.

216 Jim Barnett and Dave Hogan, "Senator Drops Effort to Block Suicide Law," *Oregonian* 15 Oct. 1998: AI.

217 "Challenges in Court, Congress," *Oregonian* 12 July 1998: AI.

218 Erin Hoover, "Suicide: Debate Will Resume in Next Session of Congress," *Oregonian* 15 Oct. 1998: BI.

219 Qtd. by Jim Barnett and Dave Hogan, "Measure to Block Assisted Suicide Appears Sidelined," *Oregonian* 7 Oct. 1998: AI.

220 Qtd. by Erin Hoover Barnett, "A Family Struggle: Is Mom Capable of Choosing to Die?" *Oregonian* 17 Oct. 1999: GI.

221 Erin Hoover Barnett, "Is Mom Capable of Choosing to Die?" *Oregonian* 16 October 1999: GI.

222 Physicians for Compassionate Care Press Release, 23 Feb. 2000: I.

223 Qtd. by David Reinhard, "In the Dark Shadows of Measure 16," *Oregonian* 31 Oct. 1999: D5.

224 Qtd. by "Killing Grandma," editorial, Brainstorm Magazine Northwest, Nov. 1999 <http://znetsolutions.com/brainstorm.nsf/614372ec75bbb bc8825678a00e3ed9> Accessed 28 Dec. 2006.

225 Steve Duin, "Kate Cheney Still Doesn't Rest in Peace," *Oregonian* 11 Nov. 1999: C1.

226 "Congress Threatens To Repeal DWD Act," *The Compassion Report* 3.3 (Fall/Winter 2000): 1.

227 Ron Wyden, "Pain Relief Act Will Cause Far More Suffering, Not Less," *Oregonian* 16 Sep. 2000 <www.oregonlive.com> Accessed 28 Dec. 2006.

228 Qtd. by Dave Hogan and Erin Hoover Barnett, "Assisted Suicide Again Targeted," *Oregonian* 11 June 1999: C1.

229 Qtd. by Ed Langlois, "Senate Prepares to Take Up Pain Relief Promotion Act," *Catholic Sentinel* 5 Nov. 1999 <http://209,238.223.166.suicide_Nov.shtml# 5> Accessed 28 Dec. 2006.

230 Qtd. by Erin Hoover Barnett, "Activists Turn Inventive to Aid Suicide Option," *Oregonian* 12 Nov. 1999: A1.

231 Qtd. by "Congress Threatens To Repeal DWD Act," *The Compassion Report* 1.

232 Ron Wyden, Testimony of US Senator Before the Senate Committee on the Judiciary Regarding the Pain Relief Promotion Act, 25 April 2000.

233 Qtd. by Steve Duin, "His Conscience Provides Solace Only for One," *Oregonian* April 30, 2000: D1.

234 Qtd. by Duin, "His Conscience" D1.

235 Josh Kardon, Chief of Staff for Senator Ron Wyden, telephone interview, 7 Sep. 2007.

236 Ron Wyden, personal interview, 20 Aug. 2010.

237 Qtd. by Jim Barnett and Dave Hogan, "Suicide Bill Feud Grows Intense," *Oregonian* 6 May 2000: A11.

238 "Don't Bully Oregon," editorial, *Oregonian* 9 May 2000: D12.

239 Qtd. by Jim Barnett, "Senate Oks Giving Rural Oregon $115 Million," *Oregonian* 7 Oct. 2000 <http://www.oregonlive.com/special/assisted_suicide/index.ssf?/news> Accessed 28 Dec. 2006.

240 Jim Barnett, "Oregon Assisted Suicide Law Hangs on Tax Bill," *Oregonian* 26 Oct. 2000: A1.

241 Qtd. by Jim Barnett, "Wyden Halts Vote on Suicide Bill," *Oregonian* 30 Oct. 2000: E1.

242 Qtd. by Barnett, "Wyden Halts" E1.

243 Congressional Record, 26 Oct. 2000: S11104.

244 Qtd. by Jim Barnett, "Suicide Law Survives One Challenge But Faces Another," *Oregonian* 16 Dec. 2000: A1.

245 Ron Wyden, "Statement Upon Defeat of Nickles Legislation to Overturn Oregon's Physician-Assisted Suicide Law," 15 Dec. 2000.

246 Jeff Mapes, "Lieberman Favors Banning Assisted Suicide," *Oregonian* 12 Oct. 2000: A5.

247 Kardon, personal interview.

248 "In Congress Nickles Pushes, Wyden Defends," *Connections* 2.1 (Fall 2000): 1.

249 Qtd. by Sam Howe Verhovek, "Oregon Chafes at Measure to Stop Assisted Suicides," *New York Times* 29 Oct. 1999: A1.

250 Ron Wyden, "Statement Upon Defeat of Nickles Legislation," 15 Dec. 2000.

Chapter 6

251 Qtd. by Bill Kettler, "Death in Family," *Mail Tribune* 25 June 2000: A1.

252 Qtd. by Bill Kettler, "Joan Lucas Left No Details," *Mail Tribune* 26 June 2000: A1.

253 "Heart of the Issue," editorial, *Mail Tribune* 28 June 2000: 12A.

254 Physicians for Compassionate Care Press Release, "Assisted-Suicide Experiment Has Failed," 19 Feb. 2001: 1.

255 "Background Check," *Oregonian* 31 Mar. 2005: A8.

256 Ed Langlois, "Medical Marijuana Ruling May Suggest Fate of Oregon's Assisted Suicide Law," *Catholic Sentinel* 25 May 2001: 1.

257 Qtd. by Jim Barnett, "State Suicide Law Waits on Bush," *Oregonian,* 11 June 2001: E8.

258 Katherine Pfleger, "Wyden Urges Bush to Lay Off Assisted Suicide Law," *Mail Tribune* 31 Oct. 2001: 5A.

259 Tom Detzel and Jim Barnett, "Wyden to Bush: Keep Hands Off Suicide Law," *Oregonian* 31 Oct. 2001: D1.

260 Sam Howe Verhovek, "US Acts to Stop Physicians Who Assist Suicides in Oregon," *New York Times* 7 Nov. 2001: A1.

261 John Ashcroft, Office of the Attorney General, Washington D.C. 6 Nov. 2001. Memorandum for Asa Hutchinson, Administrator of the Drug Enforcement Administration.

262 Erin Hoover Barnett and Ashbel S. Green, "The Reaction: State Officials and Doctors Will Challenge the Action," *Oregonian* 7 Nov. 2001: A15.

263 Oregon Right to Life Press Release on Ashcroft Ruling, 6 Nov. 2001. <www.ortl.org> Accessed 14 Mar. 2012.

264 Ed Langlois, "Catholic and Pro-Life Groups Hail Ruling to Thwart Assisted Suicide," *Catholic Sentinel* 9 Nov. 2001: A1.

265 "Oregon Law Should Stand," editorial, *St. Petersburg Times* 24 Feb. 2005 <www.sptimes.comm/2005/02/24/Opinion/Oregon_Law> 22 Sep. 2006, Accessed 28 Dec. 2006.

266 Ellen Goodman, "Ashcroft's Assisted Suicide Stance Is Simply Bizarre," *Mail Tribune* 15 Nov. 2001: 8A.

267 Ed Langlois, "Catholic and Pro-Life Groups," A1.

268 Qtd. by Christy Karras, "Terminally Ill Patients Join Fight," *Mail Tribune* 8 Nov. 2001: 3A.

269 Ashbel S. Green, "State Wins Time to Defend Suicide Law," *Oregonian* 9 Nov. 2001: A1.

270 Don Colburn, "Ailing Man Caught in Legal Limbo," *Oregonian* 8 Nov. 2001: A1.

271 Barbara Coombs Lee, ed., *Compassion in Dying* (Troutdale: New Sage Press, 2003) 87.

272 Qtd. by Susan Okie, "I Should Die the Way I Want To," *Washington Post* 1 January 2002: A1.

273 Qtd. by Mary A. Fischer, "To Live or Die," *Readers Digest* 3 May 2003 <http//www.deathwithdignity.org> Accessed 29 Dec. 2006.

274 Ed Langlois, "Judge's Assisted-Suicide Ruling Set in Context of Grueling Moral Debate," *Catholic Sentinel* 1 Nov. 2001 <http:/209.238.166/SuicideNov01.shtml#Nov23_01> Accessed 20 Dec. 2006.

275 Qtd. by Ashbel S. Green, "Ruling Adds Time to Weigh Suicide Law," *Oregonian* 21 Nov. 2001: A1.

276 *Oregon v. Ashcroft*, US District Court for the District of Oregon, CV 01-1647, Transcript of Temporary Restraining Order: 9, lines 13-20, 9 Nov. 2001.

277 Temporary Restraining Order line 19-21.

278 Qtd. by Green, "Ruling Adds" A1.

279 Ed Langlois, "Suicide Law Remains in Effect as Federal Judge Takes More Time to Decide," *Catholic Sentinel* 30 Nov. 2001: 1.

280 Qtd. by Ashbel S. Green, "State Wins Time "A1.

281 Ed Langlois, "Church Leaders Put Hopes on High Court," *Catholic Sentinel* 18 April 2002: 2.

282 *Oregon v. Ashcroft*, Permanent Injunction in US District Court for the District of Oregon. CV 01-1647-JO. 17 April 2002.

283 Green, "Suicide Law Upheld" 1A.

284 Ashbel S. Green, "Suicide Law May Go to 9th Circuit," *Oregonian* 21 April 2002: A1.

285 Qtd. by David Kravets, "Feds Go After Assisted-Suicide Law," *Mail Tribune* 24 Sep. 2002: A1.

286 Ashbel S. Green, "Ashcroft Buttresses Suicide Law Challenge," *Oregonian* 24 Sep. 2002: A1.

287 Ed Langlois, "Bishops to File Brief in Assisted-Suicide Case," *Catholic Sentinel* 27 September 2002: 6.

288 Qtd. by Ashbel S. Green, "Suicide Law Argued Today," *Oregonian*, 7 May 2003: A1.

289 Ashbel S. Green, "Judges Quiz Attorneys on Oregon Assisted Suicide Law," *Oregonian* 8 May 2003: C1.

290 George Eighmey, e-mail to the author, 22 May 2004.

291 *Oregon v. Ashcroft*, US Court of Appeals for the Ninth Circuit, CV-01-01647-JO. Opinion Argued and Submitted 7 May 2003 and filed 26 May 2004. 02-35587 D.C. 1: 6616.

292 Qtd. by Ashbel S. Green and Don Colburn, "Court Bars Ashcroft Role in Suicide Law," *Oregonian* 27 Mar. 2004: A1.

293 *Oregon v. Ashcroft*, US Court of Appeals for the Ninth Circuit, CV-01-01647-JO: 6616.

294 Ed Langlois, "Assisted-Suicide Case Seems Bound for High Court," *Catholic Sentinel* 4 June 2004: 6.

295 Langlois, "Assisted-Suicide Case" 6.

296 Barbara Coombs Lee, Compassion in Dying Federation, e-mail to author, 27 May 2004.

297 Qtd. by Adam Liptak, "Ruling Upholds Oregon Law Authorizing Assisted Suicide," *The New York Times* 27 May 2004: A1.

298 Qtd. by Colin Fogarty, "Appeals Court Upholds Death With Dignity Act," Oregon Public Broadcasting 26 May 2004.

299 Ashbel S. Green and Jim Barnett, "Assisted Suicide Under Siege in Court and Capitol," *Oregonian* 20 Feb. 2005: A1.

300 "Suicide Law Defies Prediction, Associated Press," *Mail Tribune* 9 Mar 2001: 1A.

301 N. Greg Hamilton, "Physicians for Compassionate Care Reacts to the Ninth Circuit Court of Appeals Decision," Press Release, 25 May 2004: 1.

Chapter 7

302 "One Year Later: Lessons from Terri Schiavo," Compassion & Dying Top Stories, 30 Aug. 2006 <http://cojmpassionandchoices.org> Accessed 7 May 2007.

303 Teresa Carson, "Schiavo Case Casts Spotlight on Oregon Suicide Law," Reuters 22 Mar. 2005 <http: www.deathwithdignity.org> Accessed 8 Sep. 2007.

304 Jim Barnett and Jeff Kosseff, "Schiavo Case Puts New Focus on Oregon," *Oregonian* 27 Mar. 2005: A1.

305 Don Colburn, "End-Of-Life Debate Starts Earlier, Goes Differently in Oregon," *Oregonian* 27 Mar. 2005: A1.

306 "Did Chief Justice Roberts Mislead Senator Wyden?" Blue Oregon, Open discussion. <www://blueoregon.com/2006/01/drd_Chief_Justi.html> Accessed 28 Dec. 2006.

307 Jim Barnett, "Judge's Federal Stance May Favor Suicide Law," *Oregonian* 21 July 2005: A1.

308 *Gonzales v. Oregon*, US Supreme Court, Oral Arguments before the court, 5 Oct. 2005: 14.

309 "The Supreme Court Considers Challenge to Oregon's Death With Dignity Act," The Pew Forum on Religion and Public Life, 30 Sep. 2005: 11.

310 *Ashcroft v. Oregon.* 04-623, US Supreme Court, Nov. 9, 2004. On Petition for a Writ of Certiorari, 2004 WL 2544622 (U.S.): 1.

311 Brief of the Petitioners, Paul Clement Acting Attorney General, et al., *Gonzales v. Oregon*, 64-623 in the Supreme Court of the United States, 2 Feb. 2004: iii.

312 Brief for Respondent State of Oregon, Hardy Myers, et al. *Gonzales v. Oregon*, 64-623 in the Supreme Court in support of the respondents, 18 July 2005: 21.

313 Brief for Respondents, State of Oregon, et. al., filed by Peter Rasmussen and David Hochhalter, Eli Stutsman counsel of record, 21 July 2005.

314 Brief for the Patient-Respondents, Nicholas van Aelstyn and Kathryn Tucker, *Gonzales v. Oregon*, 64-623 in the Supreme Court in support of the respondents, 10 Jan. 2005: 3.

315 Brief for the Patient-Respondents, van Aelstyn and Tucker: 36.

316 Brief, Amicus Curiae of Senators and Representatives, *Gonzales v. Oregon*, 64-623 in the Supreme Court, 11 May 2005: 2.
LifeSite Daily News 3 July 2002, Washington D.C. <www/lifesite.net> Accessed 22 Dec. 2006.

317 Catholic Medical Association, Teresa Collett, Brief Amicus Curiae, *Gonzales v. Oregon*. 64-623 in the Supreme Court of the United States, 11 May 2005: 2.

318 Ed Langlois, "Case Shows Depressed Patients Could Fall Victim to Assisted-Suicide Law," *Catholic Sentinel* 14 May 2004: 1.

319 Physicians for Compassionate Care, George Lynch counsel, Brief for Amicus, *Gonzales v. Oregon*, 64-623 in the Supreme Court in support of petitioners, 9 May 2005.

320 Ed Langlois, "Man's Assisted-Suicide Attempt Draws Attention to the Practice's Flaws," *Catholic Sentinel* 11 Mar. 2005, 1.

321 George Eighmey, e-mail to the author 22 May 2004.

322 American Civil Liberties Union, *Gonzales v. Oregon*, 64-623 in the Supreme Court in support of the respondents, 18 July 2005: 22.

323 Autonomy Inc. and Cascade AIDS Project, Amy Sabrin counsel, Brief, *Gonzales v. Oregon*, 64-623 in the Supreme Court in support of the respondents, 21 July 2005: 16.

324 Paul M. Collins, "Lobbyists Before the U.S. Supreme Court," *Political Research Quarterly* 69.1, March 2007: 65.

325 *Gonzales v. Oregon*, US Supreme Court, Oral Arguments 9.

326 *Gonzales v. Oregon*, US Supreme Court, Oral Arguments 10.

327 *Gonzales v. Oregon*, US Supreme Court, Oral Arguments 29.

328 *Gonzales v. Oregon*, US Supreme Court, Oral Arguments 36.

329 *Gonzales v. Oregon*, US Supreme Court, Oral Arguments 35.

330 *Gonzales v. Oregon*, US Supreme Court, Oral Arguments 53.

331 *Gonzales v. Oregon*, US Supreme Court, Oral Arguments 53.

332 Jim Barnett, "Court: Justices Fire Questions at Both Sides," *Oregonian* 6 Oct 2005: A1.

333 *Gonzales v. Oregon*, US Supreme Court, October Term 2005, 04-623, Majority Opinion Judge Kennedy: 2.

334 "Supreme Court's Decision in *Gonzales v. Oregon*," The Pew Research Center, Legal Backgrounder, Jan. 2006: 3.

335 "Individual Rights Win a Round," editorial, *The News Register* (McMinnville, OR) Reprinted in the *Mail Tribune*, 28 Jan. 2006: 4B.

336 *Gonzales v. Oregon*, US Supreme Court, October Term 2005, 04-623, Dissenting Opinion Judge Scalia: 4.

337 *Gonzales v. Oregon*, Dissenting Opinion of Judge Scalia: 25.

338 *Gonzales v. Oregon*, U.S. Supreme Court, October Term 2005, 04-623, Dissenting Opinion Judge Thomas 60.

339 *Gonzales v. Oregon*, Dissenting Opinion, Judge Thomas 60.

340 Don Colburn, "A Moment of Triumph," *Oregonian* 18 Jan. 2006: A8.

341 Qtd. by Linda Greenhouse, "Court, 6-3, Says Attorney General Was Wrong in Oregon Case," *New York Times* 18 Jan. 2006: A16.

342 "Disability Activists Criticize Administration," PRWeb, press release newswire,18 Jan. 2006 <http: www/prweb.com/Releases/2006/1/prwieb224213.html> Accessed 28 Dec. 2006.

343 Qtd. by Ed Langlois, "Assisted-Suicide Debate Likely to Move Back to Congress," *Catholic Sentinel* 20 Jan. 2006: 1.

344 Qtd. by Timothy Egan and Adam Liptak, "Fraught Issue, Narrow Ruling," *New York Times* 18 Jan. 2006: A16.

345 Qtd. in "US Supreme Court Rules Federal Government Does Not Have Authority to Block Oregon Physician Assisted Suicide Law," *Medical News Today* 19 Jan. 2006 http://www.medicalnewstoday.com> Accessed 28 Dec. 2006.

346 "Brownback Should Butt Out," editorial, *Mail Tribune* 18 August 2006: 5B.

347 Jeff Kosseff, "Wyden Vows Fight on Bid to Ban Assisted Suicide," *Oregonian* 14 Mar. 2005: A1.

348 Matthew Daly, "Wyden to Fight for Assisted Suicide Law," *Mail Tribune* 6 Sep. 2006: 1A.

349 Tim Christie, "Oregon Suicide Law Comes to High Court," *Register-Guard* 4 Oct. 2005: 1.

350 Marcia Angell, "Keep Alive the Right to Die," *Mail Tribune* 5 Oct. 2005: 5B.

Chapter 8

351 Qtd. by Mark O'Keefe, "Hemlock Society Director," *Oregonian* 28 June 1998: D13.

352 Janice Sanford, "Justice for Terri Schiavo," 29 May 2007, a blog at <justice1949@aol.com> Accessed 19 July 2007.

353 Eli Stutsman, Legal Council National Death With Dignity, personal interview, 8 June 2007.

354 Bradley S. Wittman, Director Election Liaison Division, Michigan Department of State, Bureau of Elections, e-mail to author, 7 Aug. 2007.

355 Daniel Hillyard and John Dombrink, *Dying Right: The Death With Dignity Movement* (New York: Routledge, 2001) 212.

356 "Ad Campaign to Fight Proposal B," *The Michigan Daily* 15 Aug. 1998 <http://www.pub.umich.edu/daily/1998/sep/09-15-98> Accessed 28 July 2007.

357 Marvin Zalman, John Strate, Denis Hunter and James Sellars, "Michigan's Assisted Suicide Three Ring Circus—An Intersection of Law and Politics," *Northern University Law Review* 23 3 (1997) 863-968.

358 Wittman e-mail.

359 Death With Dignity National Center, "Efforts in Michigan," 17 Feb. 2006 <www.deathwithdignity.org/news/news/michigan.asd> Accessed 28 July 2007.

360 Barry Kosmin and Egon Mayer, *American Religious Identification Survey* (New York: The Graduate Center of the City University of New York, 2001) Exhibit 15.

361 Stephen Ziegler and Robert Jackson, "Who's Not Afraid of Proposal B?" *Politics and Life Sciences* 2, 23.1, June 2005: 42–48.

362 Stutsman, "Political Strategy and Legal Change," 252.

363 Kosmin and Mayer Exhibit 15.

364 Sandy Thompson, Candidate Registrar, Maine Commission on Governmental Ethics and Election Practices, e-mail to author, 19 Oct. 2007.

365 "Assisted Suicide Vote Will Be on Maine Ballot," CNS News 20 May 2000, Euthanasia Home Page <http://www.euthanasia.com> Accessed 28 July 2007.

366 "Come-from-Behind Victory," National Right to Life Committee, 24 July 2000 <http:www.nrlc.org/nes/2000/NRL12/maine.html> Accessed 29 July 2007.

367 Thompson e-mail.

368 Qtd. by Physicians for Compassionate Care News, vol. 3.3, Fall 2000.

369 Melissa K. Packard, Maine Director of Elections, e-mail to author, 7 Aug. 2007.

370 Pat Omandam, "Legislature Will Consider Euthanasia," *Honolulu Star-Bulletin* 10 June 1998 <http://starbulletin.com/98/06/10/news/story3.html> Accessed 28 Dec. 2006.

371 Walter Yoshimitsu, Manager Diocesan Services, personal interview, 16 June 2003.

372 Will Hoover, "Assisted Suicide Bills Get Hearing," *Honolulu Advertiser* 24 Feb. 2002 <http://the.honoluluadvertiser.com/article/2002/Feb./24/> Accessed 28 Dec. 2006.

373 Qtd. by Richard Borreca, "Assisted Suicide Measure Could Die Early in Senate," *Honolulu Star-Bulletin* 1 Mar 2002 <http//starbulletin.com> Accessed 28 Dec. 2006.

374 Roland Halpern e-mail to author 24 July 2003.

375 Hawaii Death With Dignity Act HB2487. House of Representatives, Twenty-first Legislature, 2002, State of Hawaii.

376 Qtd. by Crystal Kokua, "Senate Kills Death-With-Dignity Bill," *Honolulu Star-Bulletin* 2 May 2002 <http://starbulletin.com> Accessed 28 Dec. 2006.

377 Qtd. by Lynda Arakawa and Kevin Dayton, "Assisted Suicide Rejected," *Honolulu Advertiser* 3 May 2002 <http//the.honoluluadvertiser.com/> Accessed 28 Dec. 2012.

378 N. Greg Hamilton, "Hawaii Rejects Assisted Suicide," Press release 2 May 2002.

379 David Shapiro, "Enact Death With Dignity," *Honolulu Advertiser* 5 Feb. 2003: 1.

380 Advertisement, *Honolulu Advertiser,* PDF file <www.hpacc.org> Accessed 28 Dec. 2010.

381 Gordon Yang, "Death With Dignity Bill Shelved," *Honolulu Advertiser* 10 Mar. 2004<http://the.honoluluadvertiser.com/article/2004/Mar/10/In/N08a.html> Accessed 28 Dec. 2006.

382 Roland L. Halpern, "Don't Despair," *Honolulu Advertiser* 12 Mar. 2004 <http//www/r\org/states/Hawaii/news-archives.org> Accessed 28 Dec. 2006.

383 Richard Brislin, "Culture Clash," *Honolulu Star-Bulletin* 2 June 2003 <http//starbulletin.com/2002/06/02> Accessed 28 Dec. 2006.

384 Jaymes Song, "Report Gives Hawaii Mixed Grades for End-Of-Life Care," *Honolulu Advertiser* 18 Nov. 2002 <http://web.lexis-nexis.com> Accessed 28 Dec. 2006.

385 "Liberty on the March," Compassion & Choices 2011 Annual Report, 2011: 6.

386 Kate Folmar, "Californians Favor Assisted Suicide," *Mercury News* 2 Mar. 2005 <MerdcuryNew.com> Accessed 28 Dec. 2006.

387 Qtd. bySteven Ertedt, "California Bill Would Legalize Assisted Suicide," *LifeNews.com,* 9 Nov. 2004: 1

388 Qtd. by Steven Harmon, "Right-to-Die Battles Look to Be Lengthy," *Contra Costa Times* 7 July 2006 <http://www.deathwithdignity.org> Accessed 30 July 2007.

389 Qtd. by James Ricci, "Right-to-Die Bill Failure Again Linked to Mistrust," *Mail Tribune* 8 Aug. 2007: 1.

390 Sandy Kleffman, "Suit Filed Over Pain Treatment of Ill Man," *Contra Costa Times* 28 Mar. 2003: A1.

391 Sandy Kleffman, "Doctor Disciplined," *Contra Costa Times* 17 Jan. 2004: A3.

392 Qtd. by Susannah Rosenblatt, "Activists Rally to Redlands Doctor's Cause," *Los Angeles Times* 12 Sep. 2006 <http://www.dwd.org/news/news/latimes> Accessed 30 July 2007.

393 John Schwartz and James Estrin, "In Vermont, A Bid to Legalize Physician-Assisted Suicide," *New York Times* 20 Mar. 2005 <http://newyorktimes.com> Accessed 28 Dec. 2006.

394 Kosmin and Mayer Exhibit 15.

395 Francis Brooks, Vermont Sergeant at Arms, personal interview, 19 July 2007.

396 Robin Lunge, Maria Royle, Michael Slater. "Oregon's Death With Dignity Law and Euthanasia in the Netherlands: Factual Disputes," Legislative Council, State of Vermont, 2004: 21.

397 Vermont Compassion & Choices <www//choicesvermont.org> Accessed 28 Dec. 2006.

398 Kenneth Angell, Statement on Vermont "Death With Dignity" Proposal 30 Jan. 2003.

399 Patient Choice and Control at End of Life Act in 2007 (H 44). VT LEG 211335.v2.

400 Michel Consejo, Vermont State Representative, personal interview, 19 Jan. 2007.

401 "Victory in the Vermont State House," Vermont Right to Life Committee 22 Mar. 2007 <www.vrlcnet/VRLCMaihfiles/VictoryOverPAShtml> Accessed 20 July 2007.

402 Ross Sneyd, "Legislature Opens Debate on Death With Dignity," Associated Press 23 Feb. 2007 <http://web.lexix-nexis.com.proxy.tui.edu/universe> Accessed 20 July 2007.

403 Ross Sneyd, "House Votes Down Assisted Suicide Bill," Associated Press 21 Mar. 2007 <http://web.lexix-nexis.com.proxy.tui.edu/universe> Accessed 20 July 2007.

404 Dick Walters, President Vermont Death With Dignity, personal interview, 18 July 2007.
405 "Oregon's Assisted Suicide Experience," Omega Publications, Salem, OR. n.d.
406 Michael Sorokin, lobbyist Vermont Death With Dignity, personal interview, 16 July 2008.
407 Qtd. by Don Colburn, "Oregon Activists Tell Washington What to Expect," Newhouse News Service 10 Jan. 2008 <http:/www/lexisnexis.com.proxy.tui.edu/us/Inacademic/frame> Accessed 12 Sep. 2008.
408 William Toffler, Physicians for Compassionate Care, personal interview, 14 Aug. 2007.
409 Eli Stutsman, "Political Strategy and Legal Change," Quill, Timothy and Margaret Battin, Eds. *Physician-Assisted Dying* (Baltimore: John Hopkins Press, 2004), 255.
410 Peg Sandeen, Death With Dignity National Center, personal interview, 15 Aug. 2007.
411 Stutsman, "Political Strategy and Legal Change," 259.
412 Barbara J. Nelson, *Making an Issue of Child Abuse* (Chicago: University of Chicago Press, 1984), 77.
413 Jack Walker, "The Diffusion of Innovations Among the States," *American Political Science Review* 63 (Sep. 1969): 895.
414 Vermont General Assembly, Hearings on S. 281, 21 January 2008, attended by author.
415 Vermont General Assembly, Act 166, Palliative Care; End-of-Life Care; Pain Management, effective date: 1 July 2008.

Chapter 9
416 Deborah Stone, *Policy Paradox* (New York: W.W. Norton Company, 1988) 11.
417 Mark Moore, *Creating Public Value* (Cambridge: Harvard University Press, (1995) 123.
418 Eli Stutsman, personal Interview, 4 June 2007.
419 Steven Ertelt, "Washington Former Governor Will Still Head Up Assisted Suicide Bill," *LifeNews* 17 Oct. 2008 <http://www.lifenews.com/bio1805.html> Accessed 26 Nov. 2008.

420 Patricia Killen and Mark Shibley, "Surveying the Religious Landscape," *The Pacific Northwest, The None Zone.* ed. Patricia Killen and Mark Silk, (New York: Rowan and Littlefield, 2004) 24.

421 Austin, Jenkins, "Supporters of Washington Assisted Suicide Decry Catholic Money," Oregon Public Broadcasting Website 14 Aug. 2008 <http://news.opb.org> Accessed 13 Sep. 2008.

422 Qtd. by Kathie Durbin, "Out-of-State Interests Spend Big," *The Columbian* 28 Aug. 2008, AI.

423 Kim Sheley, e-mail to author, 8 Oct. 2008.

424 Joseph Turner, "Voters Will Decide In November, Catholics Start Fight Against Initiative," *The News Tribune* 3 Sep. 2008: B0I.

425 Francine Barber, Homily at Blessed Theresa of Calcutta Parish, Woodville, WA. I2 Oct. 2008. <http://wwwthewccc.org> Accessed 2 Dec. 2008.

426 Bill Haines and Gina Haines, Homily at St. Louise de Marillac Church, Bellevue WA, 19 Oct. 2008 <http://wwwthewccc.org.> Accessed 2 Dec. 2008.

427 Joseph Turner and Anna Walters, "Catholic Church Solicits Money to Defeat Assisted Suicide Initiative," *Bellingham Herald* 4 Sep. 2008. <http://www.bellinghamherald.com> Accessed 26 Nov. 2008.

428 Washington State Public Disclosure Commission, database of contributions, 2008. <www.pdc.wa.gov/servlet/InitContServlet> Accessed 26 Nov. 2008.

429 Kathie Durbin AI.

430 "Death With Dignity, Approve I-I000," editorial, *Seattle Times* 8 Oct. 2008 <http://seattletimes.nwsource.com> Accessed 26 Nov. 2008.

431 William Herman, "My Life Does Not Belong To The State of Church," letter, *Seattle Times* 17 Jan. 2008 <http://seattletimes.nwsource.com> Accessed 26 Nov. 2008.

432 Death With Dignity Facts website, Northwest Passage Counseling, 2008.<deathwithdignityfacts.com/default.aspx?ID=35> Accessed 26 Nov. 2008.

433 Barbara Roberts, "Get the Facts Straight," YouTube 29 Oct. 2008<http://www.youtube.com/watch?v=LJkgBIYJuXI> Accessed 28 Nov. 2008.

434 "Doctor-Daughter," YouTube I4 Oct. 2008 <http://www.youtube.com/watch? v=LjgBIyJuXI> Accessed 28 Nov. 2008.

435 Janet Tu, "New Ads, Barbs Over I-1000," *The Seattle Times* 31 Oct. 2008 <http:seattletimes.nesource.com> Accessed 26 Nov. 2008.

436 No on I-1000 website, undated <http//www.noassistedsuicide.com.> Accessed 28 Nov. 2008.

437 Martin Sheen, "Yes on I-1000" (I-1000), YouTube 31 Oct. 2008 <http://www.youtube.com/watch?v=T-DwFmZpol/w> Accessed 11 Dec. 2009.

438 Rachel La Corte, "Washingtonians Weigh Assisted Suicide," *Mail Tribune* 15 June `2008: 4B.

439 Jonquil Frankham, "New Washington No On I-1000 Ad Features Woman Who Was Offered Assisted Suicide by Insurance Company," LifeStyleNews.com. 28 Oct. 2008 <http://groupsyahoo.com/group/private/message> Accessed 15 July 2009.

440 The Death With Dignity Report, Fall 2008: 1.

441 Washington Secretary of State, Elections, 4 Nov. 2008, General Election <http//vote.wa.gov/elections/wei/results> Accessed 26 Nov. 2008

442 Don Colburn, "Washington's Death With Dignity Isn't a Trend: Opponents and Supporters Say," *Oregonian* 7 Nov. 2008 <http://oregonlivel-com> Accessed 14 Dec. 2008.

443 I-1000 Vote By County, Washington Secretary of State, 5 Nov. 2008 <http://vote.wa.gov/elections/wei/ResultsByCounty> Accessed 30 Nov. 2008.

444 CNN News Exit Poll I-1000, Election 2008, 24 Nov. 2008 <http://www.cnn.com/ELECTION/2008/results/polls/#WAI01pl.> Accessed 9 Jan 2009.

445 Charles Bentz, e-mail to author, "Get Involved." From Physicians for Compassionate Care, 15 Oct. 2008.

446 Curt Woodward, "Former WA Gov Files Assisted Suicide Initiative," Associated Press 10 Jan. 2008 <http://www.lexisnexis.com> Accessed 1 Dec. 2008.

447 John Iwasaki, "State Second in Nation to Allow Lethal Prescriptions," *Seattle Post-Intelligencer* 5 Nov. 2008 <http//seattlepi.nwresource.com> Accessed 28 Nov. 2008.

448 Carol Ostrom, "At Least 36 Die Using Washington State's New Law," *Mail Tribune* 5 March 2010: 2A.

449 Rita Marker, Euthanasia and Assisted Suicide Task Force Website, "Assisted Suicide: The Continuing Debate," 2008. <http//wwwinternationaltaskforce.org/cd.htm.> Accessed 28 Nov. 2008.

450 Kathryn L. Tucker, "Privacy and Dignity at the End of Life: Protecting the right Of Montanans to Choose Aid in Dying," *Montana Law Review* 68.2 Summer 2007: 318.

451 Montana Constitution art II, sec 4 and 10, 6 June 1972.

452 Robert Baxter, Affidavit for the Montana First Judicial District Court, *Baxter et al v. Montana*, 28 June 2008: 3.

453 *Baxter et al v. Montana*, Montana First Judicial District Court, Lewis and Clark County, 17 Oct. 2008. Complaint.

454 Wesley J. Smith, "Suing For the Right to Assisted Suicide," 18 Oct. 2007 <www.weslyjsmith.com> Accessed 8 Dec. 2008.

455 *Baxter et al v. Montana*, Montana First Judicial District Court, Lewis and Clark County, 5 Dec. 2008. Decision and Order: 17.

456 *Baxter* Decision and Order: 23.

457 "Montana Judge: Man Has Right To Assisted Suicide," *Mail Tribune* 7 Dec. 2008: 6A.

458 "Bishop Pledges to Fight Ruling Legalizing Assisted Suicide in Montana," *The Pilot* 9 Jan 2009: 7.

459 "Liberty on the March," Compassion & Choices 2011 Annual Report, 2011:12

460 "US Supreme Court Rules Federal Government Does Not Have Authority to Block Oregon Physician Assisted Suicide Law," *Medical News Today* 19 Jan. 2006 <www/medicalnewstoday.com/medicalnews.php?newsid=36285&rfod=RSSFeeds> Accessed 28 Dec. 2006.

461 "The Next Steps to the Next State," *The Dignity Report*, (Spring 2009) I.

462 Jane Gross, "Landscape Evolves for Assisted Suicide," *The New York Times* 11 Nov. 2008: Health, 11.

Chapter 10

463 Qtd. by Don Colburn, "Why Am I Not Dead?" *Oregonian*, 4 Mar. 2005: AI.

464 Don Colburn, "Assisted-Suicide Attempt Fails," *Oregonian* 4 Mar. 2005: AI.

465 *2011 Summary of Oregon's Death With Dignity Act.* Table I <www.oregon.gov/dhs/ph/pas> Accessed 10 Mar. 2012.

466 Don Colburn, "Doctor-Assisted Suicide Cases Flat in 2005," *Oregonian* 10 March 2006: D1.

467 "The Death With Dignity Alliance," *Connections,* published by Compassion in Dying Federation, Summer 2002: 7.

468 Qtd. by Ed Langlois, "Man's Failed Assisted-Suicide Attempt Draws Attention to the Practice's Flaws," *Catholic Sentinel* 11 Mar 2005: 1.

469 Linda Ganzini, Steven Dobscha, Ronald Heintz, and Nancy Press, "Oregon Physicians' Perceptions of Patients Who Request Assisted Suicide and Their Families," *Journal of Palliative Medicine* 6. 3 (2003): 557–563.

470 Qtd. by John Schwartz and James Estrin, "In Oregon, Choosing Death Over Suffering," *New York Times.* 1 June 2004: D4.

471 Qtd. by Ganzini, "Physicians' Perceptions," 387.

472 Qtd. in "Death by Dehydration Seems Peaceful, Nurses Say," Reuters News Service, 24 July 2003 <http://www.wllspan.org/Health/News/reuters> Accessed 29 Dec. 2006.

473 Linda Ganzini, Elizabeth Goy, Lois Miller, Teresa Harvath, Ann Jackson, and Molly Delorit, "Nurses Experiences With Hospice Patients Who Refuse Food and Fluids to Hasten Death," *New England Journal of Medicine* 3494: 4 (24 July 2004): 360.

474 Ganzini, "Nurses Experiences," 360.

475 Ganzini, "Nurses' Experiences," 359.

476 Ganzini, "Nurses' Experiences," Table 3: 363.

477 Ed Langlois, "Refusal to Eat, Drink at Life's End Not Aimed at Suicide, Health Workers Say," *Catholic Sentinel* 1 Aug. 2003: 1.

478 Qtd. by Ed Langlois, "Dying Oregonians Feel Pressure to Take Their Own Lives, Suicide Study Implies," *Catholic Sentinel* 27 Sept. 2004: 1.

479 Susan W. Tolle, Virginia P. Tilden, Linda L. Drach, Erik K. Fromme, Nancy A. Perrin, and Katrina Hedberg, "Characteristics and Proportion of Dying Oregonians Who Personally Consider Physician-Assisted Suicide," *The Journal of Clinical Ethics* 15.2 (2004): 112.

480 Tolle, "Characteristics and Proportion," 115.

481 Linda Ganzini and Steven Dobscha, "Clarifying Distinctions Between Contemplating and Completing Physician-Assisted Suicide," *The Journal of Clinical Ethics* 15. 2 (2004): 121.

482 David Meir, Carol-Ann Emmons, Sylvan Wallenstein, Timothy Quill, Sean Morrison, and Christine Cassel, "A National Survey of Physician-Assisted Suicide and Euthanasia in the United States," *New England Journal of Medicine* 338.17 (1998): 1193–1201.

483 Qtd. by Langlois, "Dying Oregonians," 1.

484 Langlois, "Dying Oregonians," 1.

485 Brittany Levine, "Assisted-Suicide Study Finds No Bias Against the Vulnerable; Concerns Focus on Elderly, Poor, Minorities," *USA Today* 17 Oct., 2007: 9D.

486 Ganzini and Dobscha 121.

487 Don Colburn, "25% of Sick Who Choose Suicide May Be Depressed," *Oregonian* 8 Oct. 2008: A1.

488 Linda Ganzini. "Prevalence of Depression and Anxiety in Patients Requesting Physicians' Aid in Dying: Cross Sectional Survey," *British Medical Journal* (2008) 337: a1682.

489 Ganzini, "Prevalence" 5.

490 Steve Hopcraft, "Ganzini Depression Study Comment," *Compassion & Choices*, 6 Oct. 2008.

491 Michael Young, Ira S. Halper, David C. Clark, William Scheftner, and Jan Fawcett. "An Item-Response Theory Evaluation of the Beck Hopelessness Scale." *Cognitive Therapy and Research* 16. 5 (Oct. 1992): 579–587.

492 Ganzini, "Prevalence" 4.

493 George Eighmey, "Study Finds Dying Patients Think About Death," Compassion & Choices, October 2008.

494 George Eighmey, "Study Finds."

495 Oregon Department of Health Services News Release, 9 Mar. 2004.

496 *2011 Summary of Oregon's Death With Dignity Act* <www.oregon.gov/dhs/ph/pas> Accessed 10 Mar. 2012.

497 Qtd. by Don Colburn, "Fewer Turn to Assisted Suicide," *Oregonian* 11 March 2005: A1.

498 *2011 Summary of Oregon's Death With Dignity Act.*

499 *2011 Summary of Oregon's Death With Dignity Act.*

500 *2011 Summary of Oregon's Death With Dignity Act.* Table I.

501 Mark O. Hatfield, *Official 1997 Special Election Voters' Guide, State of Oregon,* compiled and distributed by Phil Keisling, Secretary of State: 6.

502 *2011 Summary of Oregon's Death With Dignity Act.*

503 "Physicians for Compassionate Care Education Foundation Press Release," 8 Mar. 2012.

504 "Physicians for Compassionate Care Education Foundation Press Release.

505 Ed Langlois, "Assisted Suicide Report Plagued by Shortcomings." Physicians for Compassionate Care Press Release, 23 February 2000: 2.

506 Ed Langlois, "Bias Makes Travesty of Assisted-Suicide Report," *Oregonian* 7 Feb. 2004: C4.

507 Kenneth Stevens and William Toffler, "Assisted Suicide: Conspiracy and Control," *Oregonian,* 24 Sep. 2008 <http://blog.oregonlive.com/opinion_impacct> Accessed 15 June 2009.

508 Physicians for Compassionate Care Website <www.pccef.org> Accessed 23 April 2007.

509 *2011 Summary of Oregon's Death With Dignity Act.*

510 Qtd by Don Colburn, "Assisted Suicides Increase," *Oregonian,* 19 Mar. 2008: EI.

511 Patrick O'Niell, *Eighth Annual Report on Oregon's Death With Dignity Act:* 10 <http://egov.Oregon.gov/DHS?ph/pas/> Accessed 22 April 2006.

512 Ganzini, "Prevalence," 6.

513 Linda, Ganzini, Heidi Nelson, Melinda. Lee, et al., "Oregon Physicians' Attitudes About and Experiences with End-of-Life Care Since the Passage of the Oregon Death With Dignity Act," *Journal of the American Medical Association* 2888 (2002): 91–98; and Linda Ganzini, Heidi Nelson, Teri Schmidt, Dale Kraemer, Molly Delorit, and Melinda Lee, "Physicians' Experiences With the Oregon Death With Dignity Act," *New England Journal of Medicine* 342. 8 (24 Feb. 2000): 557–563.

514 Qtd by Don Colburn, "Assisted Suicides Increase," EI.

515 Qtd. by Eli Stutsman, "Political Strategy and Legal Change." Quill, Timothy, and Margaret Battin, eds. *Physician-Assisted Dying* (Baltimore: John Hopkins Press, 2004), 199.

516 Schwartz and Estrin DI.

Conclusion

517 Ashbel S. Green, "Suicide Law Returns to Voters," *Oregonian* 10 June 1997: AI.

518 Damian Mann, "Locally Issue Gets Mixed Reviews," *Mail Tribune* 18 Feb. 2006: IA.

519 Don Colburn, "Other States See Path," *Oregonian* 22 Jan. 2006: AI.

520 Jim Barnett, "Senator Smith Ends Opposition to State's Law in Light of Ruling," *Oregonian* 18 Jan. 2006: IA.

521 Qtd. by Don Colburn, "Oregon Activists Tell Washington What to Expect," Newhouse News Service 10 Jan. 2008 <http:/www/lexisnexis.com.proxy.tui.edu/us/Inacademic/frame> Accessed 12 Sep. 2008.

522 Don Colburn, "Washington's Death With Dignity Isn't a Trend: Opponents and Supporters Say," *Oregonian,* 7 Nov. 2008 <http://oregonlivel-com> Accessed 14 Dec. 2008.

523 Qtd. by Jim Barnett and Jeff Kosseff, "Schiavo Case Puts New Focus on Oregon," *Oregonian* 27 Mar. 2005: AI.

524 Kathy Barks Hoffman, "Only Oregon Has Assisted Suicide Law," Associated Press Online, 26 May 2007 <http://wib.lexis-nexis.com.proxy.tui.edu/univers/document> Accessed 17 Sep. 2007.

525 U.S. Supreme Court, *Gonzales v. Oregon,* Oral Arguments before the Court, 14 Oct. 2005: 9.

www.ingramcontent.com/pod-product-compliance
Lightning Source LLC
Chambersburg PA
CBHW060310290526
45789CB00001B/472